Psychology of Gift-Giving

Bernd Stauss

Psychology of Gift-Giving

Springer

Bernd Stauss
Ingolstadt, Bayern, Germany

ISBN 978-3-662-66392-9   ISBN 978-3-662-66393-6 (eBook)
https://doi.org/10.1007/978-3-662-66393-6

This book is a translation of the original German edition „Das perfekte Geschenk" by Stauss, Bernd, published by Springer-Verlag GmbH, DE in 2021. The translation was done with the help of artificial intelligence (machine translation by the service DeepL. com). A subsequent human revision was done primarily in terms of content, so that the book will read stylistically differently from a conventional translation. Springer Nature works continuously to further the development of tools for the production of books and on the related technologies to support the authors.

© The Editor(s) (if applicable) and The Author(s), under exclusive license to Springer-Verlag GmbH, DE, part of Springer Nature 2023

This work is subject to copyright. All rights are solely and exclusively licensed by the Publisher, whether the whole or part of the material is concerned, specifically the rights of translation, reprinting, reuse of illustrations, recitation, broadcasting, reproduction on microfilms or in any other physical way, and transmission or information storage and retrieval, electronic adaptation, computer software, or by similar or dissimilar methodology now known or hereafter developed.

The use of general descriptive names, registered names, trademarks, service marks, etc. in this publication does not imply, even in the absence of a specific statement, that such names are exempt from the relevant protective laws and regulations and therefore free for general use.

The publisher, the authors, and the editors are safe to assume that the advice and information in this book are believed to be true and accurate at the date of publication. Neither the publisher nor the authors or the editors give a warranty, expressed or implied, with respect to the material contained herein or for any errors or omissions that may have been made. The publisher remains neutral with regard to jurisdictional claims in published maps and institutional affiliations.

This Springer imprint is published by the registered company Springer-Verlag GmbH, DE, part of Springer Nature.
The registered company address is: Heidelberger Platz 3, 14197 Berlin, Germany

Preface

There is always an occasion for gifts. Christmas and the many birthdays are, of course, the most important gift-giving occasions in Christian-based cultures, but then there are Mother's Day, Father's Day and Valentine's Day, as well as gifts for friends and family celebrations such as weddings and christenings. And in each case you are faced with the questions "What should I give?" and "What is the perfect gift in this particular case?" First, important, albeit rather general, clues to an answer are provided by an influential essay of the American consumer behaviour researcher Russel W. Belk (1996) entitled "The perfect gift", in which he describes the ideal image of a successful gift and names specific characteristics. According to this, perfect gifts are characterised, among other things, by the fact that they inspire the recipients, meet their wishes and surprise them. In the concrete individual case, such references offer however by no means always sufficient assistance. How can you inspire a niece you hardly know? How can you fulfil the wishes of an uncle who always emphasises that he has no wishes? How can you surprise a partner who specifies exactly what he or she expects as a gift? Actually, one wants to give the recipient pleasure with a gift that is as perfect as possible and thus also deepen the existing relationship emotionally. But the often unsuccessful search for the right gift initially causes the giver to be perplexed, insecure and afraid that a gift that is not only imperfect but possibly unsuccessful will have the opposite effect of what was intended, namely disappointment and anger on the part of the recipient and an emotional distancing in the relationship.

In this situation, when you think more intensively about how to find a perfect gift or at least avoid a failed one, more and more details and pitfalls come into view. The number of questions grows: Does the low price of the gift appear as evidence of low appreciation or the high price as unwanted pressure on the recipient to give an equally expensive counter-gift? What does the gift say about me, my taste and my view of the recipient? Which gifts are currently incorrect, which children can still be given chocolate, which adults can still be given books in non-gender-sensitive language? If, as at Christmas, there are several people to consider and the gift presentation is family public, how will those involved evaluate and interpret the different gifts financially and symbolically? Is money the answer or a gift certificate? And are these and other questions to be answered differently, depending on the occasion, the stage in the life cycle and the nature of the relationship between those involved?

Such recurring questions are not only the subject of individual reflection but also of research in various disciplines, with psychology playing a particularly important role. This is also obvious, since psychological factors such as motives and attitudes influence our gift-giving behaviour, and gifts trigger considerable cognitive and emotional processes in both givers and recipients, which not infrequently have a lasting impact on relationships in family and social networks. In recent years, international psychological research on gift giving has developed considerably in quantitative terms, and a large number of empirical studies have investigated gift-giving behaviour and the accompanying psychological effects in both givers and recipients in a differentiated manner. In this way, it contributes significantly to a better understanding of the complexity of the gift-giving process. Not all questions have been answered definitively so far, nor can they be. In many cases, answers sound like "it depends", but the research findings help us to understand what does matter. The aim of this book is to contribute to this by providing an insight into the current state of research in a concise form.

The presentation of findings from psychological gift research is supplemented here by short descriptions of gift episodes in fiction literature. These are not only to be understood as illustrative additions, like a nice little card to the gift, but they serve quite substantially to understand the psychological processes. When scientific psychological studies measure enthusiasm or annoyance over a gift, or the sacrifice that gift-givers make, they do so with the help of response scales. This results not only in a methodologically necessary "displacement of the word by the number" but also in a disappearance of the experience. And it is precisely this experience that fiction literature masterfully captures in artistic form. In Thomas Mann's description of the handing over of presents on Christmas Eve in the Buddenbrook house, one can immediately relate to how it feels when a child's wishful dream comes true. In Thomas Bernhard's work, you can feel the lifelong unbridled rage that wrong gifts can cause, and in O'Henry's work, you can almost experience yourself what it means and what it does when lovers sacrifice what is most important to them for a gift. In this respect, literature helps us to comprehend and understand our feelings and behaviours as givers and receivers of gifts. It thus also makes scientific knowledge more comprehensible. That is the gift of fiction to us – and to research.

Ingolstadt, Bayern, Germany   Bernd Stauss

Contents

1	Gift Giving: Joy, Duty and Frustration	1
2	Gift and Counter-Gift: The Reciprocity Rule	25
3	The Valuation of the Gift: The Recipient Decides, Not the Giver	37
4	The Financial Value of the Gift: Can't Buy Me Love?	51
5	The Emotional Value of the Gift: Empathy, Surprise, Sacrifice	59
6	Gifts as Information Media: What They Say About the Giver and the Relationship with the Recipient	75
7	Gifts in Romantic Relationships: What Enhances and What Weakens the Relationship?	85
8	Gifts to Different Recipients: Who Gets Anything at All and How Much?	107
9	Difficult Givers and Recipients: Risk Reduction Strategies	117

x   Contents

10 Cash Gifts and Vouchers: When Are They
    Taboo and When Are They Welcome?   125

11 Handling Over and Receiving the Gift:
    The Moment of Truth   137

12 Gifts and Gender: Santa Claus Is a Woman   149

13 Gifts and Culture: What Applies Globally
    and What Regionally?   161

Epilogue   177

1

Gift Giving: Joy, Duty and Frustration

"Yes, is it Christmas already?" asks Franz Beckenbauer at the end of the 1990s in a pre-Christmas commercial for a mobile phone company, a question that has since achieved the status of a saying in Germany (Wortbedeutung 2021). In the commercial, the famous footballer who became world champion as a player and coach is surprised because a gift box ('Free & Easy X-mas Set') from Santa Claus' heavenly sleigh falls into his hands. The commercial communicates the joy of the rich celebrity, who is called the 'Kaiser', about a gift and thus the expected joy of all those who will be lucky enough to receive this mobile phone as a gift at Christmas.

The question "Is it Christmas already?" is not only to be interpreted with regard to an unexpected, actually too early giving of presents. It also refers to the strange fact that every year many people are surprised to discover that Christmas is just around the corner. This is a surprise that is surprising even in light of the fact that the holiday date is known to everyone and always has been, and Christmas items have been heavily promoted in all media for weeks, if not months, and are stacked on retail shelves. Here, the question doesn't trigger joy, but pressure: "Still not all the gifts together" – "Time is running out, and I still don't have an idea". So gift giving is not only associated with joy, gift giving is also a duty, and not infrequently gift giving also triggers frustration, for example when the desired smartphone is not under the Christmas tree at all or one from the 'wrong' manufacturer.

There is almost always cause for these different feelings. After all, gift giving is a ubiquitous phenomenon in all cultures and at all times. In countries with a Christian tradition, **Christmas** naturally plays a special role. It has long been the largest and most important occasion for the consumption of gifts. In Germany, retail sales in the 2020 Christmas season amount to €103.9 billion. And this is not primarily about Christmas articles such as the 100 million chocolate Santas and St. Nicholas that the German confectionery industry delivered to retailers, or the about 30 million Christmas trees (Statista 2021c, pp. 13, 26), but primarily about gifts. On average, German consumers surveyed planned to spend €281 on Christmas gifts that year (Statista 2021c, p. 43); in Switzerland (CHF 327) and Austria (€364), the figures were even higher (Statista 2021a, p. 23, b, p. 12).

Even if the Christmas season represents a commercial highlight and in some sectors – such as those for toys and books – accounts for around a quarter of annual sales in Germany (Statista 2021c, p. 2f.), the **economic significance of gift-giving** goes far beyond this. After all, gifts are not only given at Christmas time, but throughout the year: on major occasions in life, for births and baptisms, communions and confirmations, the start of school and passing exams, engagements and weddings, birthdays, especially round and half-round ones, Mother's Day and Father's Day, anniversaries, as souvenirs for invitations and visits to the sick, or as a thank-you for a proven favour. Or just because, for no particular reason. Gift-giving thus accompanies us through the year, and throughout our lives, from the prenatal 'baby shower', an original US tradition of a special party at which it rains gifts for the expectant mother and baby, to after death, where flowers, arrangements, wreaths or money are given at the funeral to support the bereaved, or an amount is donated in the name of the deceased to explicitly named charitable institutions (Belk 1979). Despite the fact that we live in an affluent society and that many can buy almost anything, and buy it immediately, gift-giving has not lost its importance, especially since the economy has also managed to invent other gift-giving occasions such as Valentine's Day. Giving is thus a 'consumption generator' (Bögenhold 2016, p. 33), a significant economic factor whose total annual turnover was estimated years ago by the Gesellschaft für Konsumforschung (Society for Consumer Research) at €27 billion (Messe Frankfurt 2012, p. 6).

But what exactly is meant by a **gift**? In general terms, it is something that is voluntarily given to another without directly demanding anything in return – although it may well be associated with expectations of a future return, a social or psychological benefit or a change in the relationship (Komter and Vollebergh 1997). In principle, individuals, groups or organisations can be considered as givers and recipients; the gifts can be purchased or self-made products, money or vouchers, services, but also blood, organs or donations (Belk 1979). Depending on the type of donors, recipients and gifts, there can thus be very different forms, so that it makes sense to make a concretization and delimitation.

The following considerations are based on a narrow understanding limited to personal relationships, a definition described by Davies et al. (2010) as "**relational**". Givers and recipients are each individual persons or, at most, small groups of private family or friends. Only purchased or self-created products and services, money and vouchers are considered as gifts. With the reference to the private character of the relationships, it is also made clear that commercially oriented gifts between business partners ('promotional gifts') are not taken into account. Although these also have a 'relational' character in that they are used, for example, within the framework of customer relationship management to maintain personal relationships, the associated objective is not private, but quite predominantly business motivated.

With this focus on the realm of personal relationships, a distinction is made from the broad – "**transactional**" – understanding (Davies et al. 2010), which includes institutional donors and recipients as well as a variety of other types of gifts. Here, gifts include donations to charitable, social, or political organizations or unknown third parties, patronage, foundations, volunteering, blood and organ donations, sharing on social networks, and also gifts to oneself (self-gifts). Although it is plausible that some findings on private-relational giving behaviour can be usefully applied to the study of these aforementioned facts, they are so different and specific that they each require separate consideration and can be disregarded here.

It has already been shown that giving in this private-relational understanding is of great economic importance. But it is also a fundamental **social phenomenon**, in all cultures and at all times. The respective social norm system determines the duties and the scope of action of giver and taker as well as the associated psychological consequences. In view of this importance, it is no wonder that scientific research in various disciplines is concerned with the subject: anthropology and ethnography, economics and sociology, psychology and consumer behaviour research, to name only the most important (Otnes and Beltramini 1996).

The research owes essential early impulses to ethnography and anthropology, which deal with questions of social organization and cultural characteristics of delimited societies from the perspective of their members. The French ethnographer and sociologist Marcel Mauss (1990), who is considered the founder of scientific gift research, studied gift-giving in various early societies and published his findings as early as the 1920s on the question of what functions gift-giving fulfils in these societies.

In his analysis of the gift-giving behaviour of early societies, Mauss concludes that there are **three types of obligation** that permanently maintain a system of reciprocity: The obligation to give, the obligation to receive, and the obligation to reciprocate.

The obligation to give says that while we give voluntarily, we already feel obligated to give because of social norms. This was true in early societies, but it is also true today. Modern American men consider it their duty to give a gift to their beloved partner on Valentine's Day (Rugimbana et al. 2003). And not bringing a gift when invited to a birthday party or Christmas Eve is a gross violation of that obligation.

Equally binding is the second obligation to **receive a gift**. In archaic societies, refusing a gift is tantamount to a declaration of war (Mauss 1990, p. 13). But in our society, too, refusing to accept a gift on a birthday or at Christmas represents a particularly unkind, even snubbing act.

Every acceptance of a gift creates a kind of tension, a feeling of dependence on the giver. This can be reduced or resolved simply by fulfilling the third obligation, namely the **obligation to reciprocate** by giving a gift in return. In the case of reciprocal gift-giving on Christmas Eve, this tension can be immediately resolved because the obligation to reciprocate is instantly fulfilled. In other gift-giving situations, such as an invitation to a dinner party, the tension can only be resolved by a reciprocal invitation extended no later than the time of parting. However, at the 'return dinner', the first invitee also expects a guest gift if he himself brought one at the previous meeting. The tension can also only be completely resolved if the value of the gift and the counter-gift are balanced or appropriate.

This third norm, that giving and receiving should be roughly balanced, is called the **reciprocity rule**. All recipients of a gift know it. They know that in receiving it they are 'indebted', that they must 'repay', and they know that the givers know this too. That is, all parties involved know this rule, but it remains a kind of open secret because its explicit formulation is taboo (Bourdieu 1998, p. 97). This reciprocity rule will be discussed in detail in the next chapter. Here, first of all, a closer look at the obligatory nature of giving and receiving is necessary.

Because the obligation to give a gift does not mean that it is fulfilled when you hand over something. Quite the opposite: if one wants to give pleasure with the gift, the 'right' gift is required. The search is often even for the **perfect gift**, which Belk (1996) describes with the help of characteristics that show that he also includes the motivation and behaviour of the giver as well as the expectations and reactions of the recipient: The perfect gift should excite, be luxurious in that it goes beyond the merely necessary, surprise or otherwise be uniquely tailored to the desires of the recipient, the occasion and the relationship, and require special effort or sacrifice on the part of the giver.

Of course, this does not always succeed, or even rarely, but the norms of a perfect or at least right gift determine the givers' considerations in producing gift ideas and their selection decision, but also the recipients' reaction in evaluating the gift actually received (Sherry et al. 1992, 1993).

This already makes it clear that gift giving is not a moment in time, but comprises a multi-stage, complex **pro-**

cess. Various authors develop **stage models of** this process with successive phases. Wooten and Wood (2004) divide the overall process into dramaturgical acts and show that both giver and receiver are obliged to play their roles correctly in each act. However, Sherry's (1983) division of the process into the phases of "gestation", "prestation", and "reformulation" proves most influential. Following this concept, a distinction is made here – more linguistically comprehensible – between the phases or acts of 'preparation', 'handover' and 'use'.

The **first act**, '**preparation**', covers all aspects that precede the handing over and receiving of the gift. On the part of the **giver**, this involves the considerations to be made regarding the possible expectations and wishes of the recipient, the internal and external search activities and the weighing of alternatives, also taking into account the **giver's** own motives, expectations and financial resources. In addition, there is the gift decision, the purchase and the preparation of the acquired product for the gift. Of course, givers have to observe a variety of standards in the process. They must know and consider the interests and tastes of the recipients. Otherwise, their spontaneous and/or later reactions will show them that they have missed their target and violated clear social norms. Thus, the object to be given must be appropriate, but it must also have the prescribed character of a gift: The giver must remove or paste over price tags before giving, and gifts must be properly wrapped and possibly labeled with special cards or stickers (Belk and Coon 1993). Even if a bottle of wine is judged appropriate and proper as a host gift, it seems inappropriate to hand it to a host without a tote bag or other packaging. In the special case of a gift of flowers, on the other hand, a different standard applies; there, the paper wrapping must be removed before handing it over, unless it was a paper sleeve.

The **recipients** also have obligations already in the preparation phase, especially if there is frequent social contact between the parties involved. They must give signals regarding their gift expectations. This can be done by explicitly naming an unambiguous wish or by subtle hints that give the giver the chance to guess the supposedly 'secret' wishes and leave room for manoeuvre for the concrete gift alternative. At the same time, the potential recipient must reflect on the giver's expectations and resources to avoid frustration arising at this stage. If donors get the impression from the recipient's signals that they are dealing with a particularly demanding, difficult-to-satisfy or otherwise complicated recipient (Otnes et al. 1993), negative emotions will already dominate in the first act.

The **second act**, '**handover**', is about the exchange itself, giving and receiving, and the interpersonal communication dynamics that take place. Personal handover in particular always involves a minimum of ritual or ceremonial activity (Sherry 1983), and the norms of verbal and non-verbal communication must be adhered to. The **giver** has to present the gift with a personal salutation – referring to the occasion if necessary ("This is for you"; "Happy birthday"; "Thank you for inviting me"). He or she also has to follow the moment of unwrapping with attention (Belk and Coon 1993).

The **recipient** decodes the messages associated with the gift, the value and appreciation expressed in the gift itself, in the type and care of the packaging and in the style of presentation. And regardless of what positive or negative emotions these messages trigger, the recipient has a duty to respond correctly in every case. This includes first showing anticipation, and after realizing exactly what the gift is about, reacting with surprise, delight, enthusiasm and gratitude. And not just in words, but also in body language. Facial expressions must match the words. Receipt of a bottle of wine must be accompanied by interested questioning and showing, and not by careless putting away. The less the recipient's actual pleasure, the better his or her acting must be in this act, because otherwise he or she is signaling to the giver that the gift is actually unwanted or disliked. Any uninvolved or disappointed reaction on the part of the recipient will be correctly deciphered by the giver and can affect the relationship just as negatively as the failed gift already does on the part of the recipient.

The **third act**, 'use', shows how the recipient deals with the gift. If the gift disappears through consumption, as in the case of food – such as the contents of a classic gift basket – this stage is mostly unproblematic. 'Mostly' refers to the overwhelming majority of cases where the recipient's tastes are catered for, rather than, say, the vegan being given a liverwurst and the diabetic being given a box of chocolates. Unsuccessful gifts of this kind are hardly ever forgotten. The successful gifts, on the other hand, remind people of the occasion when they consume them, and the feeling of happiness when eating strengthens the relationship.

The situation is different if the gift is an accessory for the home: a picture, a vase, a porcelain figurine, a photo calendar. If there are recurring contacts, such as family contacts, the giver expects the gift to remain visible or at least to be kept and displayed in the living area. If the gift meets the taste and expectations of the recipient, the constant contact with the object is also a reminder of the giver, which strengthens the relationship. But if it does not, the object is a permanent and repetitive nuisance to the recipients who are obliged to present it. In this case, if they seek to avoid the annoyance and stow the gift on the basement shelf, regift it, or dispose of it, this triggers disappointment and anger in the giver, who misses his gift as invisible. Even if the lack of appreciation is supposedly not so noticeable because a self-knitted scarf is never worn, a book remains unread on the shelf or a personal photo book is never picked up again, this is still often registered by the giver. In all these cases, the signal of failure to give is clear, and this has consequences. Giver and receiver see each other with different eyes, the relationship is weakened, and uncertainty about future gift-giving behaviour increases.

This gift-giving process or 'gift-giving drama' also makes it clear how strongly our apparently voluntary gift-giving is determined by rules, and it will be shown later that the mentioned here only represent the basic rules. It also becomes clear that the whole process is or can be connected with **strong emotions**, strong positive but also strong negative feelings (Ruth 1996; Ruth et al. 1999, 2004).

Positive feelings include, above all, joy and satisfaction, contentment, gratitude and affection, for both exchange partners. Many givers already look forward to please someone else with their gift during the preparation phase. They enjoy putting themselves in the recipient's shoes, coming up with ideas, and setting out to find a suitable gift. They enjoy making something themselves, getting gifts, wrapping and writing accompanying cards. Above all, they look forward to the outcome of their activities: the recipient's joy when they receive the gift, their surprise, their excitement. And they are especially happy in the exchange phase if they really succeed in triggering joy, enthusiasm and/or gratitude in the recipient. This reciprocal positive emotional effect is reinforced when the recipient confirms his or her joy in the use phase by appreciatively handling the giver's gift.

Obviously, however, not all people are equally capable of joy in giving, since certain **personality traits** of the giver have a strong influence on whether joy arises and what kind of joy it is. One important trait is **empathy**. In particular, empathic people are motivated in the preparation phase to create or find something that will trigger a particularly positive feeling in the recipient at the moment they receive the gift. The empathic person wants to maximize the recipient's pleasure and in doing so feels "altruistic" joy (Sherry 1983, p. 160), which makes it easy for him or her to comply with gift norms.

However, there is apparently a second – almost opposite – form of pleasure in gift giving, which Sherry (1983, p. 160) calls "agonistic", but which can probably be more accurately named with the term 'egoistic'. The **selfish**, who are only concerned with their own interests, do not primarily want to maximise the recipient's pleasure, but their own. It is easy for them to violate gift norms as long as this serves to increase their own pleasure, for example if they can use the gift to show off their financial superiority, their supposedly superior taste or a special talent. This egoistic pleasure is therefore at the expense of the recipient and to the detriment of the relationship and is only considered here in connection with unsuccessful gift-giving behaviour.

Whether people tend to feel altruistic or agonistic pleasure is apparently dependent on different fundamental **values**. This is shown by an international comparative study of gift-giving behaviour in four countries of Western culture – the USA, France, Germany and Denmark – (Beatty et al. 1996), whereby the results are consistent across all the countries studied and across generations and genders. According to these findings, altruistic giving is associated primarily with values oriented toward warm interpersonal relationships; selfish giving, on the other hand, is typical of people with self-centered values. Accordingly, people with strongly relationship-oriented values give more often and make more effort than those who are primarily focused on themselves and their enjoyment of life.

These findings are supported by more sophisticated studies on the influence of emotions in the preparation phase of gift-giving behavior, based on the psychological approach of the **Appraisal Tendency Framework** (Lerner and Keltner

2000, 2001; Han et al. 2007). De Hooge's (2014, 2017) research demonstrates that the effects of emotions on donor intentions can be explained by two appraisal dimensions: the valence of the emotion in terms of the extent to which the giver feels positive or negative emotions, and the causality of the emotion, i.e., whether the giver caused the emotional event himself or the receiver did (De Hooge 2014, 2017). The studies show that givers always increase their giving activities when they feel positive emotions. The opposite is true for negative emotions, unless they caused them themselves, and gifts appear to be a useful tool to preserve and strengthen the relationship in this situation. In addition, they examine how the effects of the valence and causality appraisal dimensions on gift-giving behavior depend on the personality trait 'Interpersonal Orientation'. Strongly interpersonally oriented givers are highly motivated to develop and enhance interpersonal relationships and to be responsive to others, whereas givers with low interpersonal orientation are primarily concerned with maximizing their own advantage. If one considers the research results only with regard to positive emotions, it becomes apparent that highly interpersonally-oriented people intensify their giving behaviour when positive emotions are caused by the recipient, while for donors with a low interpersonal orientation the causality of the emotion does not play a role.

Other studies show that further value attitudes influence the pleasure of giving, such as hedonism and self-determination (Passos et al. 2020). Not all research findings are always in complete agreement regarding such influencing factors, but there is agreement regarding the consequences. More empathic or altruistic pleasure in giving influences the givers' behaviour at all stages of the gift-giving process: it increases the extent to which the givers engage with the potential desires and expectations of the recipient, the extent of their search and procurement activities, and their care and attention during gift delivery.

In considering the duties associated with gift giving, it has already become clear that the overall process is by no means associated solely with positive feelings. On the contrary, gift giving is a very ambivalent emotional experience. In their study, published under the title "The dark side of the gift", Sherry et al. (1993) draw attention to an aspect that is often overlooked in the joyful glow of gift-giving, namely the **negative emotions** in the gift-giving process – an aspect to which scientific research is paying increasing attention (Sherry et al. 1993; Ruth et al. 2004; Marcoux 2009).

In the **preparation phase**, when one first thinks about a suitable gift, one often already feels a considerable degree of perplexity, uncertainty and doubt. The obligation to give a gift often triggers stress and anxiety (Larsen and Watson 2001; Wooten 2000). One feels overwhelmed, the fear creeps in of not having an idea for the right gift, making a poor choice, and disappointing the recipient with the wrong gift and thus failing as a giver (Sherry 1983; Otnes et al. 1994; Flynn and Adams 2009). These negative emotions can be exacerbated by a variety of other factors, such as the nature of the relationship. An example of this is the situation of a new family member faced with the task of finding gifts for members of a family network, where the aim is to avoid upsetting anyone despite extensive unfamiliarity with expectations, needs and traditions. Davies et al. (2010, p. 415) describe the anxious situation of a new wife who has to find a suitable gift for her mother-in-law, while she also has to host the family Christmas for the first time.

Perplexity and fears do not decrease in the phase of gift selection and procurement. On the contrary: Especially in the context of 'last minute shopping' the pressure increases further. And if one fails in the search for the perfect or right gift in the preparation phase, the only way out to reduce the negative emotions is to ask the recipient directly about his or her wishes. What is unreservedly recommendable with regard to children proves to be ambivalent with regard to gifts for adults. The direct inquiry reduces the risk of a wrong choice towards zero, but in many cases makes the gift giving banal and boring for the giver, which emotionally negatively accompanies the positive feeling of relief to have escaped the decision compulsion (Sherry et al. 1993). At the same time, the direct query of wishes also puts the receiver in an ambivalent emotional position. On the one hand, he or she will be pleased to have avoided an unsuccessful gift and to have a wish fulfilled; on the other hand, the direct query may also be interpreted as a clear sign of a lack of thoughtful effort on the part of the giver and, together with the lack of surprise, may cloud the pleasure.

The fulfilment of explicit wishes can also trigger negative feelings in the givers for other reasons, namely if the desired object goes completely against their central attitudes, values and taste preferences. From consumer research, we know that people tend to choose products for themselves that correspond to their self-image and thus serve to confirm their own identity (Gao et al. 2009). Now, when they buy products not for themselves, but as gifts for others and want to align with the recipients' desires, it happens that they have to make divergent choices. And in some cases, they find themselves in the situation of having to choose products that run counter to their own identity if they want to fulfil the wishes of the recipient. A supporter of the Borussia Dortmund football club finds it difficult to give away a fan article of the rival club Schalke 04. Someone who prefers Bauhaus-style crockery will not like to give a service with floral decorations. Those who prefer fact-based non-fiction books are reluctant to give a bestseller of a populist opinion-maker as a gift.

1 Gift Giving: Joy, Duty and Frustration

Ward and Broniarczyk (2011) have examined this situation using the example of the election problem in the use of wish lists. These are drawn up by recipients for an upcoming event and contain a catalogue of products available for purchase from a particular retailer or online. Such lists are an essential part of the ritual at weddings, enabling the new couple to begin constructing a family identity and expressing it in the form of gifts (Bradford and Sherry 2013). For the givers, such wish lists reduce the effort of gift-seeking, but also limit their freedom of choice. Thus, for a variety of reasons, they may be forced to buy something from the given list that contradicts their own identity. Other givers may have already selected less problematic gifts and remaining alternatives are out of the question due to price. In their empirical studies, the authors find that the thus forced purchase of an identity-contradicting gift for a good friend is perceived by the givers as an identity threat, since the recipient appears to be virtually part of themselves due to the close relationship. In this situation, two contradictory cognitions exist for the givers: On the one hand, the knowledge of correctly fulfilling an explicit wish of the recipient, and on the other hand, that the choice of the gift does not correspond to their own identity and that they therefore misrepresent themselves. This leads to efforts to restore the shaken self-image. They therefore tend to place particular emphasis on identity-enhancing products in subsequent purchases for themselves. However, this changes little the negative emotions associated with the gift choice, which are exacerbated when the gifts are presented openly in a wider circle.

This already addresses the fact that strong negative emotions can of course also occur in the **handover phase**. At the moment of truth, when the gift is received and unwrapped, negative emotions such as disappointment, frustration, anger, embarrassment or sadness can be felt by both givers and recipients. As just mentioned, for givers even a quasi-public gift-giving can be perceived as disturbing, for example at Christmas or on the occasion of a birthday party, where not only the recipient can compare the different gifts, but also all those present make these comparative assessments. The author Florian Illies impressively describes such a situation.

> **Florian Illies: Anleitung zum Unschuldigsein (Guide to Being Innocent)**
>
> The protagonist is invited to a friend's birthday party and portrays the threatening thoughts and negative emotions that can arise during a public gift exchange: Fear that the chosen gift will appear to the other guests as completely incomprehensible, since they do not know the personal considerations; shame and a guilty conscience, because a gift certificate that was self-made at the last minute under time pressure reveals one's own carelessness and, moreover, is given in the knowledge that it will probably not be redeemed; uncertainty as to how the observing other guests will interpret the gift in terms of the personality of the giver; disappointment and embarrassment when one sees that the host is just unwrapping a book that one oneself is about to hand over as a gift (Illies 2002, pp. 225–226).

Negative emotions are even stronger, of course, when a gift turns out to be unsuccessful because it does not suit the recipient's tastes and interests or even contains an unpleasant message (e.g., receiving an 'etiquette book' from one's mother-in-law). While there is a strong social norm for recipients to suppress and disguise these negative feelings, this does not change their often persistent existence and subsequent effects on the relationship. The same is true for the disappointment of the givers who, despite the recipient's best efforts to control his or her negative feelings, cannot escape the fact that their well-intentioned gift has failed, and who store this failure in long-term memory (Sherry et al. 1993).

Whether the gift is spontaneously gratifying or not, the moment of reception is also the moment when the obligation becomes conscious and the reciprocity rule begins to affect the recipient's psyche. It is this ambivalence that leads the Italian sociologist Pierpaolo Donati (2003, p. 246) to point out a curiosity in the vocabulary of Indo-European languages: "the word *gift* has a dual semantic content which in English means to give freely but in German has taken on the meaning of 'poison'". This is the poison of the negative feelings of having been unwillingly pushed into a relationship of dependency and guilt (Ruth et al. 1999). This can go so far that recipients see the acceptance of the gift as so stressful that they look for ways to detoxify themselves and escape from the 'straitjacket of social expectations' (Marcoux 2009, p. 671) as soon as possible.

The **use phase** can also be associated with short-term and long-term negative emotions. Seemingly short-term are the disappointments about a wrong gift, if the decision can be revised, for example by return or exchange with free new choice by the recipient. In online retail, this is not a problem if the order is placed at short notice before the gift is given, as there is generally a 14-day cancellation period. Brick-and-mortar retailers usually offer the option of exchange as a gesture of goodwill, and for a long time the days after Christmas seemed virtually reserved for the return and exchange of unwanted gifts (Caplow 1984, p. 1313). However, for some time now the exchange rate has been falling in the face of the increase in cash and gift voucher gifts – to around 5% at present in Germany across all product ranges (HDE 2020). In the case of the returning or exchanging recipients, the relief at having corrected a wrong gift usually dominates, but they will hardly or just not gratefully associate the joy over the newly acquired product with the giver. In any case, the giver's own misconduct remains incriminating in his or her memory.

The consequences for the recipient are even more problematic if an unloved gift cannot be undone due to certain, usually family, considerations and remains visible in the living environment as a permanent source of annoyance. At least in the medium term, such a gift is usually withdrawn from everyday view after all, ends up in the cellar and is often kept there for a long time before it is thrown away or destroyed (Rucker et al. 1992). But even then, unsuccessful gifts are far from being completely disposed of from memory and do not simply disappear. At the latest when a new round of gift-giving is due, it is very likely that the memory of the disappointing experience will reappear (Marcoux 2009).

A seemingly sensible alternative to this destruction of value would be to pass on the unwanted gifts to other people who might appreciate them more. Although there is much to be said for this idea, because it is a sustainable, resource-saving and value-preserving measure, it is largely frowned upon and even constitutes a social normative taboo (Adams et al. 2012). The reason lies in the plausible assumption that such giving away is perceived by the original giver as insulting, hurtful, and an expression of a lack of appreciation, since the recipient does not only disregard the gift, but also the giver (Schmied 2006, p. 68). Knowing this, many recipients refrain from re-gifting or decide to do so with a guilty conscience and feelings of ingratitude, or choose this alternative only after an appropriate time lag, when the negative feelings have subsided.

However, Adams et al. (2012) assume that there is an asymmetry in the perceptions of givers and recipients with regard to the estimation of re-gifting. They suggest that recipients overestimate the negative reactions of the giver, thus falsely assuming the giver's expectations that their gifts will be appreciated to be stronger than they actually are. The empirical results of their studies confirm the assumption that recipients find re-gifting more offensive than givers and that recipients overestimate the extent to which givers feel offended by re-gifting. In addition, recipients find re-gifting as offensive as destroying or throwing away the gift, while givers clearly find these behaviors more offensive.

These results are argumentatively well comprehensible and empirically proven. However, no hasty conclusions should be drawn from them. The fact that recipients overestimate the negative assessment of the donors does not mean that this negative assessment of the donors is irrelevant. Moreover, important influencing factors remain unconsidered, such as the closeness of the relationship between the parties involved and the type of gift. It is conceivable, for example, that in very close relationships of kinship and friendship, re-gifting is perceived as particularly hurtful, especially when it involves gifts with a high symbolic value that have required great sacrifice on the part of the giver (such as jewellery) or have been personally created with a great deal of effort (such as a hand-knitted scarf). Here, the disrespect signaled by re-gifting is sure to lead not only to negative emotions on the part of the giver, but to strain on the relationship as a whole. Initiatives for special re-gifting days to make re-gifting easier and more acceptable take this into account. For example, the etiquette rules for National Regifting Day in the US strongly recommend against re-gifting a gift that was of special significance to the original giver or is homemade or personalized. It also advises against returning the gift to the original giver (!) (National Day Calender 2020).

Even if recipients adhere to such rules and can also be sure that the giver cannot find out about the passing on or even approves of it, this course of action should not be viewed solely through the rose-tinted glasses of sustainability and value preservation. On the one hand, many recipients are first and foremost happy to get rid of the unloved gift and the passing on accompanies the positive feeling of relief with the nice feeling of the supposed good deed. However, they are often not concerned with pleasing others but with finding victims. Therefore, they often choose people to pass on who they look down on, for example because they have a lower social status, and think the products are suitable for them, possibly taking the perspective of the original giver. They also choose a situation where they do not expect reciprocity because of the difference in status. This allows them to avoid receiving a comparatively failed object in return for the unwanted gift (Sherry et al. 1992).

References

Adams G et al (2012) The gifts we keep on giving: documenting and destigmatizing the regifting taboo. Psychol Sci 23(10):1145–1150

Beatty SE et al (1996) An examination of gift-giving behaviors in four countries. In: Otnes C, Beltramini RF (eds) Gift giving: a research anthology. Bowling Green State University Popular Press, Bowling Green, pp 19–36

Belk RW (1979) Gift giving behavior. In: Sheth JN (ed) Research in marketing, Bd 2. JAI Press, Greenwich, pp 95–126

Belk RW (1996) The perfect gift. In: Otnes C, Beltramini RF (eds) Gift giving: a research anthology. Bowling Green State University Popular Press, Bowling Green, pp 59–85

Belk RW, Coon GS (1993) Gift giving as agapic love: an alternative to the exchange paradigm based on dating experiences. J Consum Res 20(3):393–417

Bögenhold D (2016) Schenken als Konsumgenerator. In: Bögenhold D (ed) Konsum: Reflexionen über einen multidisziplinären Prozess. Springer VS, Wiesbaden, pp 33–36

Bourdieu P (1998) The economy of symbolic goods. In: Bourdieu P (ed) Practical reason. Polity Press, Cambridge, pp 92–123

Bradford TW, Sherry JF (2013) Orchestrating rituals through retailers: an examination of gift registry. J Retail 89(2):158–175

Caplow T (1984) Rule enforcement without visible means: Christmas gift giving in Middletown. Am J Sociol 89(6):1306–1323

Davies G et al (2010) Gifts and gifting. Int J Manage Rev 12(4):413–434

De Hooge IE (2014) Predicting consumer behavior with two emotion appraisal dimensions: emotion valence and agency in gift giving. Int J Res Mark 31(4):380–394

De Hooge IE (2017) Combining emotion appraisal dimensions and individual differences to understand emotion effects on gift giving. J Behav Decis Making 30(2):256–269

Donati P (2003) Giving and social relations: the culture of free giving and its differentiation today. Int Rev Sociol 13(2):243–272

Flynn FJ, Adams GS (2009) Money can't buy love: asymmetric beliefs about gift price and feelings of appreciation. J Exp Soc Psychol 45(2):404–409

Gao L et al (2009) The 'shaken self': product choices as a means of restoring self-view confidence. J Consum Res 36(1):29–38

Han S et al (2007) Feelings and consumer decision making: the appraisal-tendency framework. J Consum Psychol 17(3):158–168

HDE Handelsverband Deutschland (2020) Weihnachtsgeschenke im Lockdown: Regelungen für Gutscheine und Umtausch. https://einzelhandel.de/presse/aktuellemeldungen/13103-weihnachtsgeschenke-im-lockdown-regelungen-fuer-gutscheine-und-umtausch. Accessed 10 Feb 2021

Illies F (2002) Anleitung zum Unschuldigsein. S. Fischer Verlag, Frankfurt a. M

Komter A, Vollebergh W (1997) Gift giving and the emotional significance of family and friends. J Marriage Fam 59(3):747–757

Larsen D, Watson JJ (2001) A guide map to the terrain of gift value. Psychol Mark 18(8):889–906

Lerner JS, Keltner D (2000) Beyond valence: toward a model of emotion-specific influences on judgement and choice. Cogn Emot 14(4):473–493

Lerner JS, Keltner D (2001) Fear, anger, and risk. J Pers Soc Psychol 81(1):146–159

Marcoux J-S (2009) Escaping the gift economy. J Consum Res 36(4):671–685

Mauss M (1990) The gift: the forms and reason for exchange in archaic societies. Routledge, London

Messe Frankfurt (2012) Management Report ‚So schenkt Deutschland'. https://ambiente.messefrankfurt.com/content/dam/messefrankfurt-redaktion/ambiente/general/management-reports/2017/manrep-schenken-deutschland.pdf. Accessed 8 Feb 2021

National Day Calender (2020) National re-gifting day – Thursday before Christmas. https://nationaldaycalendar.com/national-re-gifting-day-thursday-before-christmas/. Accessed 10 Feb 2021

Otnes C, Beltramini RR (1996) Gift giving and *gift giving*: an overview. In: Otnes C, Beltramini RF (eds) Gift giving: a research anthology. Bowling Green State University Popular Press, Bowling Green, pp 3–15

Otnes C et al (1993) Gift selection for easy and difficult recipients: a social roles interpretation. J Consum Res 20(2):229–244

Otnes C et al (1994) In-laws and outlaws: the impact of divorce and remarriage upon Christmas gift exchange. Adv Consum Res 21:25–29

Passos SC et al (2020) Personal values and gift giving act: a proposed connection. Estudios Gerenciales 36(155):218–228

Rucker MH et al (1992) Thanks but no thanks: rejection, possession and disposition of the failed gift. Adv Consum Res 19:488

Rugimbana R et al (2003) The role of social power relations in gift giving on Valentine's day. J Consum Behav 3(1):63–73

Ruth JA (1996) It's the feeling that counts: toward an understanding of emotion and its influence on the gift-exchange processes. In: Otnes C, Beltramini RF (eds) Gift giving: a research anthology. Bowling Green State University Popular Press, Bowling Green, pp 195–214

Ruth JA et al (1999) Gift receipt and the reformulation of interpersonal relationships. J Consum Res 25(4):385–402

Ruth JA et al (2004) An investigation of the power of emotions in relationship realignment: the gift recipient's perspective. Psychol Mark 21(1):29–52

Schmied G (2006) „Expansion des Ich, das sich…im Schenken ausströmt". Identität, Funktion, Status, Gefühl als soziologische Komponenten des Schenkens. In: Rosenberger M et al (eds) Geschenkt – umsonst gegeben? Gabe und Tausch in Ethik, Gesellschaft und Religion. Peter Lang, Frankfurt a. M., pp 65–84

Sherry JF (1983) Gift giving in anthropological perspective. J Consum Res 10(2):157–168

Sherry JF et al (1992) The disposition of the gift and many unhappy returns. J Retail 68(1):40–65

Sherry JF et al (1993) The dark side of the gift. J Bus Res 28(3):225–244

Statista (2021a) Weihnachten in der Schweiz. https://de.statista.com/statistik/studie/id/31438/dokument/weihnachten-in-der-schweiz-statista-dossier/. Accessed 25 Feb 2021

Statista (2021b) Weihnachten in Österreich. https://de.statista.com/statistik/studie/id/31498/dokument/weihnachtenin-oesterreich-statista-dossier/. Accessed 25 Feb 2021

Statista (2021c) Weihnachtsgeschäft in Deutschland. https://de.statista.com/statistik/studie/id/7662/dokument/weihnachten-statista-dossier/. Accessed 8 Feb 2021

Ward MK, Broniarczyk SM (2011) It's not me, it's you: how gift giving creates giver identity threat as a function of social closeness. J Consum Res 38(1):164–181

Wooten DB (2000) Qualitative steps toward an expanded model of anxiety in gift-giving. J Consum Res 27(1):84–95

Wooten DB, Wood SL (2004) In the spotlight: the drama of gift reception. In: Otnes CC, Lowrey TM (eds) Contemporary consumption rituals: a research anthology. Lawrence Erlbaum Association, Mahwah, pp 213–236

Wortbedeutung (2021) Ja, is' denn heut schon Weihnachten. https://www.wortbedeutung.info/ja_is'_denn_heut_schon_Weihnachten. Accessed on 8 Feb 2021

2

Gift and Counter-Gift: The Reciprocity Rule

Our understanding of the functions of gift-giving is largely based on early ethnographic and anthropological research, particularly the studies of Mauss (1990 [1923/1924]) and Malinowski (1984 [1922]) among archaic peoples in the Pacific island groups of Melanesia and Polynesia, and among indigenous tribes in Northwest America. They describe and explain gift-giving as a self-sustaining system of reciprocity that primarily serves to secure relationships. That is, one gives gifts to those on whose support one depends but whose assistance one cannot take for granted (Caplow 1984). There is a reciprocal relationship between the material transaction of gift giving and the social relationship. The US anthropologist Marshall Sahlins sums this up as follows: "If friends make gifts, gifts make friends" (Sahlins 1972, p. 186).

This moment of reciprocity is evident in the aforementioned duties of giving and receiving and, in particular, of reciprocating by giving a gift in return, which is called the principle of reciprocity or the reciprocity rule. This rule is the focus of social science research based on ethnography, especially economic, sociological and psychological research on gifts, which is dominated by **exchange theory**.

In the general exchange-theoretical approach of the social sciences, especially sociology, all human interactions are understood as exchanges (Thibaut and Kelley 1959; Homans 1974). They are understood as strategic interactions that occur because the participants expect to gain some advantage from them. In this sense, one gives something to someone in return for something received in the past or something expected in the future. Accordingly, give and take must balance each other out; the values received and the values given must correspond. The reciprocity thus addressed suggests applying the general exchange theory to the special case of giving (Sherry 1983).

In the exchange-theoretical discussion of gift-giving, two variants can be distinguished, depending on what is to be understood by the exchanged value, namely the economic and the social exchange theory.

In the perspective of **economic exchange theorists**, it is about the **objective price** of the gift. Gifts are valued according to their financial value: the higher the price of the gift, the more valuable it is. According to the reciprocity rule, an expensive gift puts the recipient under financial pressure. The recipient feels obliged to make an equally expensive counter-gift. For only then is a balance restored in the relationship, and the negative feelings of being dependent and still owing something disappear. Until then, however, the psychological tension remains and possibly the worry about a future financial burden, which can significantly reduce the joy of the gift received.

The basic validity of the reciprocity rule in various cultural circles is undisputed. Undoubtedly, however, there are also deviations, namely intentional violations of this norm as well as socially accepted exceptions.

2 Gift and Counter-Gift: The Reciprocity Rule

Conscious violators of the rule include the "agonistic" (Sherry 1983) or egoistic donors who seek to maximise their economic advantage in the exchange of gifts. Donors who adopt this perspective seek "negative reciprocity" (Sahlins 1972, p. 195), want to receive more than they give, so are intent on walking away from the gift process with a profit (Belk and Coon 1993). They will weigh up what level of investment in a relationship seems worthwhile in their deliberations at the preparation stage, taking into account the likely value of a return gift. When exchanging gifts, they will calculate whether the gift partner has also spent as much as they have, and they will always feel dissatisfaction if they have the impression that they have invested relatively too much. Satisfaction they feel therefore just not in the value balance of the gifts, but in the imbalance, which is expressed in the higher value of the received. However, only those people can really enjoy this pleasure who, because of their self-love, are completely insensitive to the negative consequences that their actions have on the relationship with the person involved.

Such egoists cannot even be stopped by arrangements and agreements that attempt to ensure the economic-value reciprocity of gift and counter-gift by specifying a limit or target price. This applies, for example, to the anonymous gift-giving system '**Secret Santa**', where each member of a group brings in a gift that is not supposed to exceed a fixed price, and then receives one of the other gifts by lot. Group members who are solely concerned with their economic advantage – even within the given small financial framework – can proceed completely unabashedly in the darkness of anonymity. They then choose an existing, old and unloved item – a tawdry travel memento or an obviously read and dusty paperback – and are delighted when they have drawn a more valuable gift. Their joy, moreover, appears unclouded because the intent to overcharge a friend cannot be attributed to them personally. The unhappy recipients of a worthless gift, however, will be annoyed, possibly making assumptions about the giver, but cannot direct their dissatisfaction at any particular person in the group.

More significant than these deliberate violations of the reciprocity rule are **the socially permitted exceptions** to its application. Variants of the exchange theory approach, namely work in fairness and equilibrium theory, point to such exceptions (Adams 1963). These also emphasize that when a benefit is received, a quid pro quo is necessary to establish a sense of fairness or psychological equilibrium. But they also show that and under what conditions it is possible to deviate from the norm of reciprocity. The factors to be taken into account are the capabilities and possibilities of the reciprocating exchange partner as well as the nature and intensity of the relationship between the participants.

The reciprocity rule applies to a large extent without restriction in **relationships at eye level**, for example in the relationship between roughly equal friends, but also acquaintances from the wider social network (Joy 2001). If someone receives an expensive bottle of wine from a friend for birthday and 'returns the favour' on the next occasion with an apparently cheap drink, the balance is violated. The rule loses its validity, however, if givers know of the friend's limited financial resources. In this case, they will be satisfied with a smaller return gift because they are aware that an object of comparable price would have been too great a budgetary burden for the friend.

In **family relationships**, the norm of reciprocity in gift-giving remains fundamentally valid. At the family Christmas, for example, each recipient usually has a gift for the giver as well; and parallels in value often emerge (Cheal 1986). But a fully "balanced reciprocity" (Sahlins 2013, p. 148) is neither necessary nor appropriate. For one thing,

2 Gift and Counter-Gift: The Reciprocity Rule

in many cases the dependence felt through gifts is not perceived as a burden but as a welcome moment of bonding, for example, an expensive gift as a gladly accepted recognition. For another, relationships in a family are also not balanced (Caplow 1984; Belk and Coon 1993). For example, there is still an expectation that all those who participate in feasting and gift-giving on Christmas Eve will also participate by giving gifts to others. It is also part of the expectation that life partners have at least one Christmas gift for each other. The same is true for children and parents and grandparents and grandchildren. A conditional exception to the obligation exists only for young children, but they are usually encouraged to give at least one symbolic gift and in this way are familiarised with the reciprocity rule at an early age.

But the gifts do not have to correspond in value at all. This is particularly evident with regard to gifts for **children**. It is not only common for parents to give more valuable and larger gifts to their minor children and to the adult children still living at home than they themselves receive from them. Basically, substantially more gifts flow from the older to the younger generation (Caplow 1982). With respect to **young children**, the common and widely accepted imbalance is also evident in the fact that gifts from children – viciously characterized by economist Camerer (1988, p. 198) as "often charmingly homemade and ugly, with no direct utility value to parents" – are happily accepted. When the parental givers completely obscure their own role and assign the gift-giving blessing to the Christ Child or Santa Claus, reciprocity seems to be completely canceled. However, it should not be overlooked that even today some parents make the hoped-for wish fulfilment dependent – at least as a threat – on the child's good behaviour, which must be proven in advance, as a quid pro quo. Insofar as this is the case, Santa Claus, as the "greatest of all givers", with his ability to grant or refuse rewards, serves parents as an instrument of control and surveillance (Schwartz 1967, p. 4).

But even between **partners, as well as parents and their adult children**, no attention is usually paid to equivalence of values (Caplow 1984). This is also not so necessary because, in the case of close family relationships and a long history of mutual giving, there are often already clear ideas about what is to be expected. This also includes the fact that people learn from experienced imbalances and adjust their behaviour accordingly.

However, one should not think that gift-giving in the sense of an economically interpreted exchange is therefore unproblematic in the family context. The opposite is the case. Family relationships are not only shaped by the 'gift history', but above all by experiences of perceived and deeply felt gradations, supposed preferences and demotions. These are sensations that can be deepened or weakened by gift-giving behaviour. In sibling gift-giving, an expensive gift from the sister to the brother who is not doing so well may further the relationship. It shows that she wants to give him a special treat, cares about him, and understands him (Dunn et al. 2008). However, the large gift from the successful sister may also be interpreted by the brother as further evidence of her demonstrative superiority and proof of his own failure, leading to considerable upset. In addition, families have further differentiated gift rules which relate to the respective position in the family network and which must be observed if discord is to be avoided. These rules will be discussed in detail later.

The economic view of gift exchange is, however, only one perspective, and one that cannot fully grasp the complex event. For the value of a gift can consist in something quite different from its price. This is pointed out by representatives of **social exchange theory**. They emphasize that gifts derive their meaning from their **symbolic value**, their

2 Gift and Counter-Gift: The Reciprocity Rule

significance for the relationship between giver and receiver, their expressiveness for the emotional closeness of the parties involved. In this view, the value of a gift increases with its symbolic content (Belk and Coon 1993). This is reflected in the empathy shown in identifying supposedly 'secret' wishes, in the effort and time spent in searching for or creating a gift, or in the sacrifice associated with the gift.

In the light of social exchange theory, the reciprocity rule says something different than in the economic approach. A recipient will not feel primarily obligated to return something of comparable financial value, but will feel pressure to make a reciprocal gift of comparable symbolic value (Belk and Coon 1993).

Gifts with a high symbolic value are usually only given in the context of close relationships, for example in dating or family contexts. Therefore, violations of this norm are particularly problematic. Anyone who, as the giver, has put a great deal of thought, heart and effort into a gift that is intended to symbolically illustrate emotional closeness will be particularly disappointed by a counter-gift that, in its unkindness, has an almost opposite symbolic content. However, in long-term personal relationships, psychological mechanisms also become effective that make it possible to reduce the emotional and cognitive tensions due to an unbalanced symbolic reciprocity. These include that an initially very disappointed recipient uses the donor's well-known personality-based lack of empathy as an explanation. Also, a giver who is aware of the symbolic inferiority of his or her gift may reduce the cognitive tension generated by inwardly reducing the symbolic value of the received (Belk 1976).

In principle, therefore, the reciprocity rule applies both to gifts with primarily economic value and to those with symbolic value. However, there is much to suggest that the obligation to give a reciprocal gift is perceived more intensively in the case of symbolic gifts than in the case of economic gifts, since the givers involve and reveal themselves much more in the gift and the gift reflects the relationship between the partners to a greater extent. In addition, the extent of perceived reciprocity obligation is determined by a number of other factors. For example, perceived obligation increases with the recipient's level of satisfaction, i.e., the happier the recipient is with the gift received, the more he or she perceives himself or herself to be indebted. The social expectation framework of the occasion also plays a role. In the case of socially determined occasions for gifts such as Valentine's Day, birthdays or Christmas, deviating from the reciprocity rule is not only individually problematic, but downright socially deviant behaviour. The situation is different when it comes to personal gifts that are given on individual impulse without a predetermined occasion (Antón et al. 2014).

From the perspective of exchange theory, in both the economic and the social model, the participants appear as independent partners who try to obtain a roughly equal financial or symbolic countervalue for their gift. This self-interested perspective is realistic in many cases, but it by no means does justice to all cases of gift-giving. For this reason, Belk and Coon (1993) extend the exchange theory perspective to include another type, that of **altruistic gift-giving**.

They call the approach "agapic love paradigm". Agapic love plays a major role in romantic relationships, but also in the love between close relatives (parents, children, grandparents, siblings). In terms of gift-giving, this agapic love is expressed by gifts being given without self-interest, selflessly, and without expectation of anything in return (Belk and Coon 1993). Here the reciprocity rule completely loses its meaning.

Unselfish gift-giving manifests itself in various ways. It becomes clear when gifts demonstrate that one recognizes

2 Gift and Counter-Gift: The Reciprocity Rule

and appreciates the beloved partner in his or her uniqueness and also senses his or her specific needs and desires, even if they are not expressed. It is an equally clear signal when the gift illustrates the giver's willingness to do quite a lot for the loved one, even to make personal sacrifices, just to please the other person. And such altruistic gifts often have a strong emotional impact. For example, gift research shows that recipients experience particularly high levels of satisfaction with a gift when it is obvious that it is being given without expectation or hope of a return gift (Belk and Coon 1993).

The following episode from Paul Auster's novel "The Locked Room", the third part of his "The New York Trilogy", provides a wonderful example of unselfish gift-giving between friends. In it, the 'giver' 'gives' the 'receiver' the opportunity to show up at a birthday party with a present. And the episode at the same time illuminates different perspectives on the perception of the reciprocity rule.

> **Paul Auster: The Locked Room, part three of The New York Trilogy**
>
> The narrator is invited with his friends Fanshawe and Dennis to a birthday party of a mutual friend. However, Dennis has no gift, which makes him very uncomfortable. Fanshawe recognizes this immediately and gives Dennis his gift, in such a matter-of-fact way without any gesture of pity that Dennis can accept it without feeling embarrassed. While the narrator is deeply impressed by this altruistic act, Fanshaw's mother is not at all thrilled about it later. She points out to her son that his behavior is rude and hurtful to her, since she paid for the gift and now stands in a bad light as well. Fanshawe, however, stands by his behaviour and emphasizes that he would act that way again next time (Auster 1998).

This fiction episode also points to a phenomenon that is often overlooked in the scientific discussion of altruistic giving, namely the possible different perspectives of the giver and the taker. From the perspective of the giver Fanshawe, the reciprocity rule is suspended; he expects nothing in return. The recipient Dennis, however, does not need to share this perspective; he might, for example, interpret the action in terms of the reciprocity norm and feel correspondingly obligated, if not humiliated. Although this did not occur in this case, it was initially considered possible by the narrator as a reaction. In principle, the fact that the giver does not expect anything in return does not invalidate existing relations of power and dependence – on the contrary, "dominance is all the greater where no return can come" (Corrigan 1989, p. 530). This can result in a paradoxical situation: "There is no gift that brings a higher return than the free gift – the gift given with no strings attached. For that which is truly given freely moves men deeply and makes them indebted to their benefactors" (Gouldner 1973, p. 277). To avoid such unwanted feelings of guilt, unselfish giving requires not only generosity but also sensitivity on the part of the giver, as Fanshawe demonstrates in Paul Auster's story.

Unselfish gift-giving also exists when there is no question of love or friendship and when there are no personal relationships at all. This circumstance stands outside the relational understanding of gifts that forms the conceptual framework of these considerations. But its mention at this point seems more than justified, since it refers to the Christmas story, which provides the basis for Christmas gift-giving. The three wise men from the Orient take toils and hardships to deliver their expensive gifts: gold, frankincense and myrrh. But what is important is not primarily the price of the gifts, but their symbolic content, with which they express their humble devotion. And they give unselfishly, without a thought of a worthwhile gift in return. Thus giving makes pleasure not only to the receiver but also to the giver.

References

Adams JS (1963) Towards an understanding of inequity. J Abnorm Soc Psychol 67(5):422–436

Antón C et al (2014) The culture of gift giving: what do consumers expect from commercial and personal contexts? J Consum Behav 13(1):31–41

Auster P (1998) The New York trilogy: city of glass, ghosts, the locked room. Faber and Faber, London

Belk RW (1976) It's the thought that counts: a signed digraph analysis of gift-giving. J Consum Res 3(3):155–162

Belk RW, Coon GS (1993) Gift giving as agapic love: an alternative to the exchange paradigm based on dating experiences. J Consum Res 20(3):393–417

Camerer C (1988) Gifts as economic signals and social symbols. Am J Sociol 94 (Supplement: Organizations and institutions: Sociological and economic approaches to the analysis of social structure):180–214

Caplow T (1982) Christmas gifts and kin networks. Am Sociol Rev 47(3):383–392

Caplow T (1984) Rule enforcement without visible means: Christmas gift giving in Middletown. Am J Sociol 89(6):1306–1323

Cheal D (1986) The social dimensions of gift behavior. J Soc Pers Relat 3(4):423–439

Corrigan P (1989) Gender and the gift: the case of the family clothing economy. Sociology 23(4):513–534

Dunn EW et al (2008) The gift of similarity: how good and bad gifts influence relationships. Soc Cogn 26(4):469–481

Gouldner AW (1973) The importance of something for nothing. In: Gouldner, AW For sociology. Allen Lane, London, pp 260–299

Homans GC (1974) Social behavior: its elementary forms, 2nd edn. Houghten Mifflin Harcourt, New York

Joy A (2001) Gift giving in Hong Kong and the continuum of social ties. J Consum Res 28(2):239–256

Malinowski B (1984) Argonauts of the western Pacific: an account of native enterprise and adventure in the Archipelagoes of Melanesian New Guinea. Waveland Press, Prospect Heights

Mauss M (1990) The gift: the forms and reason for exchange in archaic societies. Routledge, London

Sahlins M (1972) Stone age economics. Aldine-Atherton, Chicago

Sahlins M (2013) On the sociology of primitive exchange. In: Banton M (ed) The relevance of models for social anthropology. Routledge, London/New York, pp 139–236

Schwartz B (1967) The social psychology of the gift. Am J Sociol 73(1):1–11

Sherry JF (1983) Gift giving in anthropological perspective. J Consum Res 10(2):157–168

Thibaut JW, Kelley HH (1959) The social psychology of groups. John Wiley & Sons, New York

3

The Valuation of the Gift: The Recipient Decides, Not the Giver

The most violent, albeit usually suppressed, conflicts in connection with gift giving occur when the giver and the recipient have different assessments of the value of the gift. This begins with regard to the question of what should be considered a value in the first place. The two most important categories for the evaluation of a gift have already been presented in the context of the reciprocity rule, namely the objective value, which can be read off from the price, and the symbolic value, recognisable by the degree of empathy, effort expended, time invested and sacrifices made by the giver, as well as the degree of surprise that the gift triggers.

In addition, the usefulness, i.e. the **utility value of** the gift is to be considered. This aspect can play a role both as a motivation of the giver and in the evaluation by the recipient. However, it could be disregarded in connection with the reciprocity rule, since the receipt of a gift with a high utility value need by no means lead to an obligation to make a counter-gift with a comparable utility value.

Donors often opt for gifts with a high utility value with the motivation to provide the receiving household with useful items that they believe are still lacking. While such gifts to satisfy material needs and a certain redistribution of resources are of high importance in traditional societies and times of need, in modern societies they have only a secondary role (Cheal 1996). On a larger scale, useful objects are mainly given as gifts when new stages of life begin, such as when a new household is to be established with marriage or an existing one is to be better equipped (Wolfinbarger and Yale 1993). In this case, gifts with utility value are highly welcome, as can be seen from the fact that brides and grooms often create corresponding wish lists so that they can achieve the desired level of equipment and avoid duplicate gifts. Similarly, useful gifts are normally desired at the birth of a child, where a lot of new equipment, clothing and furniture needs to be procured. In the absence of a specific occasion, this also applies to items that meet an acute need expressed by the recipient – such as a bag for the new laptop – or enable better practice of a known hobby – such as a camera – (Larsen and Watson 2001). In these cases, the recipient's evaluation of useful gifts is positive. In other cases, where more valuable alternatives in terms of price and symbolic value are considered, valuation discrepancies may also arise between givers and receivers with respect to this value category, which are discussed below.

A **first discrepancy** between the valuations of givers and receivers occurs when the assessments differ with regard to the **amount of** the respective financial, symbolic, or utility **value.** For example, it is conceivable that recipients underestimate the price of what they have received because they do not realize that the bottle of wine given is not a run-of-the-mill product from a discount store, but a long-matured top-quality wine from a high-class vineyard. Likewise, it can happen that a high symbolic content felt by the giver remains undiscovered by the receiver because he or she is not aware of the time and effort the giver has spent searching for a suitable gift. A comparable evaluation gap opens up when givers consider the utility value of a gift to be objectively very high, for example that of a special electric tool, but the recipients consider this value to be low because they neither have the desire nor the corresponding skills to use the tool.

A **second discrepancy** occurs when the parties involved use fundamentally **different value categories** when assessing the gift. For example, a man may regard his gift – such as an expensive kitchen appliance – as particularly valuable because of its high price or high utility value, whereas the female recipient, who expected a gift with a high symbolic value, hardly notices the high monetary expenditure but does notice the lack of symbolic value. Wolfinbarger (1990) describes an equivalent situation for a failed gift. In her study, a woman reports that she was not at all pleased by her boyfriend's gift of a cappuccino machine. On the contrary, she interpreted the gift as evidence that he no longer considered her sexy.

An analogous case of discrepancy occurs when the donor gives a gift that has great symbolic value for him or her, but appears almost worthless to the recipient, who might have preferred a monetary gift or a useful gift in kind. To a father, a silver napkin ring with engraving that has been handed down in the family for generations may seem a valuable possession, especially symbolically. Accordingly, he part with it with difficulty and sees passing it on to the son as a great gift. But if the son has no sense of family connections and no use for napkins, the conflict cannot be avoided. Thus, giver and receiver apply discordant rules of valuation (Schiffman and Cohn 2009), which leads not only to dissatisfaction but also to uncertainty about what reciprocity means in these cases and how to restore psychological balance.

In all the cases mentioned, one fundamental insight becomes clear: of course, both the giver and the receiver evaluate the value of a gift, but whether the goal of pleasure and satisfaction is achieved depends solely on the receiver's evaluation. And a major cause of valuation discrepancies and conflicts lies in the fact that the **givers**, in their gift considerations and decisions, **orient themselves** primarily or solely **to their interests, their ideas or their taste**, and either do not perceive the ideas of the recipient or deliberately ignore and disregards them. If one gives a book as gift and is guided solely by one's own literary tastes, and, in choosing an article of furniture, follows only the rules of taste of one's own social milieu, there is only hope for achieving satisfaction by chance.

It is even more problematic when **donors disregard the recipient's wishes, which are known to them**. The reasons for this can be manifold. For example, the wish for a saucepan, which is geared toward practical use, may seem too trivial a gift to them. They may also have the well-meaning intention of changing the other person's behavior or attitudes, or directing their interests elsewhere. Again, it seems purely coincidental if these intentions of the giver succeed. In many cases, however, they will produce dissatisfaction. A person who needs a saucepan will often not particularly value an art print; a lover of art will not necessarily become a cook through a cookbook, and not every lover of fishing will become a friend of poetry through a book of poems.

Parents should also consider this knowledge when it comes to gifts for their **children**. Of course, educational considerations are permissible and valuable. With children, it will always be about finding something that encourages them, that increases confidence and trust in their ability to perform and that awakens new interests. Gifts give the child important clues in terms of identity, who he or she is and what the parents think he or she should be like. They convey values in terms of education, competition, possessions and aesthetics, for example. They are also used consciously or unconsciously to communicate gender roles and identities (Belk 1979). Accordingly, parents either choose toys to reinforce traditional roles by giving their sons 'typically male' toys (such as diggers, fire engines or knight castles) or their daughters 'typically female' objects (such as dolls, bracelets or pony farms), or attempt to thwart these gender stereotypes by choosing gifts that deviate from them. Since role understandings are also shaped outside the family, the latter strategy is not without risk, however. Anyone who thinks they are doing the boy who wants a plastic Playmobil pirate ship a favour in terms of gender-correct education by giving him a wooden doll's kitchen instead is likely to miss the educational objective and spoil the birthday or Christmas party.

Generally speaking, the dominant orientation towards one's own norms, interests, tastes and values only signals selfishness and egoism and thus the opposite of what gift-giving is actually about. In the worst case, this can lead to disaster, as is the case in Ludwig Tieck's novella "Weihnacht-Abend" ("Christmas Eve").

> **Ludwig Tieck: Weihnacht-Abend (Christmas Eve)**
>
> In his novella "Weihnacht-Abend" ("Christmas Eve"), Ludwig Tieck, a Romantic poet, describes the fate of a woman who lives impoverished with her daughter near the large Christmas market in Berlin. Among the blows of fate experienced by the woman is the news that her first son Heinrich has not survived the sinking of his ship in the South Seas.
>
> The son had left the parental home after a tangible dispute with the father, which came about because Heinrich did not gratefully accept the gifts chosen by the father with plan, but brusquely rejected them. The father, who had always dreamed of an academic career, now wants to realize this dream in his son and makes him a large number of expensive scholarly books as a gift. However, the son's interests

> are clearly not directed towards academia. Therefore, he does not react enthusiastically at all to the many academic works presented but informs his father that he cannot use the books, since he sees his future not at the university, but in trade and adventure. Thereupon the father reacts with an outburst of rage and violence. He throws the heaviest book at his son's head and maltreats the injured boy with blows and kicks. No wonder the son left the parental home after this incident and did not return during his father's lifetime.
>
> But Tieck's tale is a Christmas story, and that is why a "Christmas miracle" also happens on Christmas Eve: the son who was believed dead has survived and recognizes his mother at the Christmas market in his hometown. He seeks her out, is able to fulfil the little sister's previously illusory Christmas wishes and leads the family out of poverty (Tieck 2002).

The recommendation to donors to base their gift decision on the expected evaluation by the recipient is extremely plausible and intuitively obvious. After all, the gift is intended for the recipient, should bring him pleasure and be of use to him. This can best be achieved with a gift that reflects the wishes, interests and preferences of the recipient. However, this requires correspondingly precise knowledge, which in many cases is not available. In addition, systematic **misjudgement of the recipient's wishes** can occur.

This is shown by empirical studies on discrepancies in perspectives when donors are faced with the question of which of several possible gift ideas they should realize that have different advantages and disadvantages. Here, for reasons of simplification, the problem is usually limited to two gift alternatives A and B, where gift alternative A proves superior with respect to one evaluation criterion, but gift alternative B proves superior with respect to another.

In their research, Kupor et al. (2017) examine the situation of a donor who is faced with a choice between alternatives that differ according to the extent to which they are 'complete' or 'desirable'. Alternative A is the desirable gift, which the recipient would prefer, but whose price exceeds the donor's budget, so that the recipient must contribute a part. Variant B is one that the recipient also likes, though not as much, and is within the giver's price range, so it can be given in full. An example of this situation is a voucher for a restaurant with an amount sufficient for a usual dinner for two ('complete'), or for a more expensive restaurant where it is expected that the recipient will have to pay extra when visiting ('desirable'). The empirical studies show that givers prefer complete gifts because they assume that recipients perceive an incomplete gift as less appreciative, as 'half-hearted'. In contrast, however, respondents as recipients prefer the desirable gift alternative. Accordingly, donors systematically misjudge recipients' preferences and make suboptimal gifts in this regard. Whether this conclusion can be unreservedly agreed with will be discussed critically in the context of the further studies on asymmetrical assessments of donors and recipients presented below.

Baskin et al. (2014) examine a different choice situation. Here, a giver has to choose between gift certificate alternatives that differ with respect to the two criteria 'desirability' and 'feasibility'. He or she wants to give a restaurant voucher as a gift, but does not know the recipient's favourite restaurant. The giver only knows that the recipient prefers food at 'Italian'. For example, he or she may give a voucher for a better quality Italian restaurant some distance away, or for a slightly lower quality restaurant that is more easily accessible. The authors theoretically justify their assumption that gift givers who put themselves ostensibly in the recipient's shoes give greater weight to desirability attributes in their selection, while recipients give greater weight to usability and value it more highly. Thus, in the example given, they believe that the giver is likely to have a greater preference for the high quality restaurant, which is more complicated to seek out, while the recipient would have been more pleased with the more accessible but somewhat lower quality option. This assumption is confirmed in a series of empirical experiments. Thus, the authors also come to the conclusion that it is precisely the gift decision that proves to be wrong, which is oriented towards the supposed needs of the recipient. Accordingly, when there is a conflict of goals between desirability and feasibility, they recommend that donors first consider what they themselves would prefer in the role of recipient and behave accordingly, which usually means choosing the 'more feasible' variant.

Teigen et al. (2005) also investigate in their experimental studies whether givers and recipients prefer gifts that are more 'luxurious' or 'more useful', whereby 'luxurious' is to be understood in the sense of higher quality and 'useful' primarily in the sense of quantitative advantages. In the example studied, the question is whether they consider an expensive bottle of wine or instead two bottles of an average wine to be better gifts. The respondents' evaluations are by no means consistent. On the contrary, there is an asymmetrical evaluation depending on the giver's and recipient's point of view, a phenomenon known as 'preference reversal'. When asked which gift alternative they would like to give and which they would like to receive, comparable subjects in the role of the recipient opt for the 'more useful' (quantitatively superior) variant, while subjects in the role of the giver opt for the 'more luxurious' (qualitatively superior) variant.

In all the comparative studies presented, it is empirically proven that donors who make an effort to give recipient-oriented gifts in the sense of a change of perspective just do not achieve maximum satisfaction and an intensification of the relationship, but rather make the wrong decisions. The researchers offer several explanations as reasons for this. For example, gift-givers may be more interested in the recipient's spontaneous enjoyment of a complete and high-quality gift than in the recipient's long-term satisfaction with the object. It is also conceivable that givers must be more attuned to cultural gift-giving conventions because, after all, they – unlike recipients – make their preferences public with the gift. Thus, it is neither a lack of empathy or ill will nor errors in the recipient's assessment that are responsible for this decision, but rather an interest in spontaneous pleasure and respect for conventions.

However, doubts can be raised as to whether there are really wrong decisions here. Although there is no reason to doubt the empirical results, **concerns can** be raised about **the methodological design of the studies**. Most problematic is the survey design, which requires donors and recipients to evaluate gift alternatives in a pairwise comparison. For this situation is unrealistic with respect to the recipient. Indeed, givers and recipients apply a very different mode of evaluation in real life. Whereas the giver has a multitude of alternatives and choices when making a gift decision (including, should I choose the bottle of more expensive wine or would I rather choose two bottles of slightly lower quality wine?), the recipient evaluates the gift received alone. When recipients are asked to evaluate the alternatives individually rather than in a pairwise comparison, i.e., only the single bottle received or only the two lower-quality bottles, recipients' preference patterns change toward a higher evaluation of the exclusive gift items. When valued individually, complete, exclusive, immaculate gifts have undeniable advantages. In this respect, it makes perfect sense for givers to choose them and, for example, choose the gift certificate for the superior quality Italian restaurant. That recipients, if they had to evaluate the alternatives in terms of their long-term satisfaction, might have made a different choice is immaterial. Not only for the giver, but also for the recipient, the spontaneous evaluation, the joy at the moment of reception is decisive.

However, since there is always the difficulty of meeting the recipient's wishes exactly and wrong decisions are often unavoidable, gift research is increasingly concerned with the question of whether giver-centred gifts also have advantages and whether there are situations and constellations in which it is possible or advisable to deviate from the recommendation of recipient orientation.

A major **advantage of giver-centered gifts** is seen in the fact that it is much easier for givers to find a gift that reflects important aspects of their own personality than that of the recipient. And this function of gifts as a mirror of the donor's personality appears to be an advantage for the recipient. For example, Paolacci et al. (2015) provide evidence that recipients particularly value gifts when they are a very special match to the characteristic traits of the giver, i.e., there is congruence between the gift and the giver. However, this evidence is only provided in comparison with gifts with lower gift-giver congruence, while no statement is made about how the valuation turns out in comparison with a gift that is geared to the wishes and needs of the recipient.

Such comparisons are carried out by Aknin and Human (2015), and they hypothesize that a gift that reveals the giver's personality also has positive effects on the relationship with the recipient and increases the feeling of connection. The reason they see for this is that the giver opens up and makes himself or herself vulnerable with such a gift, which increases the intimacy of a relationship, especially in romantic relationships. In order to test this hypothesis, they examine in six empirical studies with different methodologies whether gifts that are oriented towards the recipient (recipient-centered gifts) or gifts that reflect the giver (giver-centered gifts) have a stronger effect on promoting closeness among the participants.

First, all six of the comparative studies confirm the expected: respondents in a nationally representative survey overwhelmingly said they would rather give a gift that reflects their knowledge of the recipient than a gift that expresses their true self. Similarly, they clearly favored preferring to receive a gift that reflects their interests and passions rather than the interests and passions of the giver. Surveys of subjects' preferences and actual gift-giving behavior on Valentine's Day again show a strong preference for recipient-centered gifts. However, studies of the influence of giver-centered and recipient-centered gifts on perceived increases in relationship closeness show a divergent result. Giver-centered gifts, with which the giver reveals an important part of his or her true personality (such as a book of favorite poems) or something they both enjoy and can spend time together with, prove to be more effective in strengthening the relationship. According to this study, while people have a strong preference for gifts that match the interests and passions of the recipient, gifts that reflect the interests and passions of the giver seem to exhibit stronger bonding effects. At least, this is said to be true for romantic or other already established relationships. Consequently, the authors conclude from the study results that gifts that focus on the giver are an often untapped resource to foster social relationships.

At first glance, this result is surprising, as it contradicts the thesis of the necessity of recipient-oriented gifts. At a second, closer look, however, the contradiction is not so clear or is resolved. Participants in the studies were asked general questions about recipient-oriented and giver-oriented gifts, and aspects of different value categories or different assessments of the amount of value did not play a role. Nor was the case of apparent disregard for the recipient's wishes considered. Moreover, the giver-centered gift was defined in a very restrictive way, namely as a special case of a gift intentionally chosen in relation to the relationship, revealing a disclosure of personality or expressing a desire to spend time and togetherness with the other. Here, gift decisions are indeed made from the giver's perspective, such as an invitation to an event of a sport that the giver loves but to which the recipient has not yet had access. Of course, gaining that access and experiencing the event together with the giver can be valuable for the recipient and the relationship. But the relationship effect of a special case proven here is by no means a license for thoughtless self-interest in gift giving.

Before donors jump to conclusions from such scientific findings, they should rather rely on traditional experiential knowledge, such as that conveyed in the animated series 'The Simpsons'. In the ninth episode of the first season, 'Life in the Fast Lane' (also known as 'Jacques to Be Wild')', Homer Simpson gives his wife Marge a bowling ball for her 34th birthday, engraved with his name and with holes fitted to his throwing hand. Unsurprisingly, this donor-centric gift triggers a serious marital crisis, even though, or perhaps because, it says so much about the personality and interests of the giver (Simpsons 2021).

References

Aknin LB, Human LJ (2015) Give a piece of you: gifts that reflect givers promote closeness. J Exp Soc Psychol 60:8–16

Baskin E et al (2014) Why feasibility matters more to gift receivers than to givers: a construal-level approach to gift giving. J Consum Res 41(1):169–182

Belk RW (1979) Gift giving behaviour. In: Sheth JN (ed) Research in marketing, Bd 2. JAI Press, Greenwich, pp 95–126

Cheal D (1996) Gifts in contemporary North America. In: Otnes C, Beltramini RF (eds) Gift giving: a research anthology. Bowling Green State University Popular Press, Bowling Green, pp 85–97

Kupor D et al (2017) Half a gift is not half-hearted: a giver-receiver asymmetry in the thoughtfulness of partial gifts. Personal Soc Psychol Bull 43(12):1686–1695

Larsen D, Watson JJ (2001) A guide map to the terrain of gift value. Psychol Mark 18(8):889–906

Paolacci G et al (2015) Give me your self: gifts are liked more when they match the giver's characteristics. J Consum Psychol 25(3):487–494

Schiffman LG, Cohn DY (2009) Are they playing by the same rules? A consumer gifting classification of marital dyads. J Bus Res 62(11):1054–1062

Simpson Wiki (2021) Der schöne Jacques. https://simpsons.fandom.com/de/wiki/Der_schöne_Jacques. Accessed 20 Mar 2021

Teigen K et al (2005) Giver-receiver asymmetries in gift preferences. Brit J Soc Psychol 44(1):125–144

Tieck L (2002) Weihnacht-Abend. Insel-Verlag, Frankfurt a. M

Wolfinbarger MF (1990) Motivations and symbolism in gift giving behaviour. Adv Consum Res 17:699–705

Wolfinbarger MF, Yale LJ (1993) Three motivations for interpersonal gift giving: experiential, obligated and practical motivations. Adv Consum Res 20:520–526

4

The Financial Value of the Gift: Can't Buy Me Love?

The fact that the price of a gift is not always decisive for the satisfaction of the recipient has already been mentioned, and also the fact that many people value the symbolic value more highly than the financial value. However, this does not mean that the price does not play a role, especially since the price also has a symbolic value. But this can be very different.

If someone of known good financial standing gives away an obviously **cheap item**, he cannot expect joyful gratitude. And this is true not only because the gift is of little financial value, but because it is interpreted as a symbol of low regard for the recipient and as an expression of a miserly character. If, on the other hand, someone gives a gift that involves a financial sacrifice for him or her, despite limited means, this symbolises generosity and a willingness to make sacrifices as well as special closeness for the recipient (Larsen and Watson 2001).

The case is more complicated when a **lot of money** is spent on a gift. In this case, a giver assumes that the amount of money spent will be rewarded accordingly, i.e. that there is a positive correlation between the price paid and the appreciation of the gift by the recipient as a result. This applies all the more if it is to be assumed that the recipient would neither be willing nor able to spend so much money on a corresponding object or event. Such an assumption seems plausible not only in economic terms but also in symbolic terms: the giver demonstrates the willingness to invest in a relationship, and he or she therefore believes that the expensive gift provides a particularly strong signal of the perceived depth of the relationship.

Various **empirical studies** provide evidence that donors do indeed adopt this perspective (Camerer 1988; Flynn and Adams 2009). However, they also show that the donor perspective does not necessarily correspond to the perspective of the recipients, indeed that there are often divergent assessments here.

Flynn and Adams (2009) examine perceptions of financial value comparatively from the donor and recipient perspectives in three studies. In the first two studies, subjects are asked about their own experiences as givers and receivers; the third uses an experiment with a hypothetical gift scenario.

The first study focuses on the gift of an engagement ring. At the time of the study, more than 80% of engagement gifts in the United States were a ring with a diamond. In this respect, it is an object that is chosen and presented with care, given its high price and the significance of the occasion. The ring gift is thus associated with both a strong emotional moment and the aspect of financial value, which makes it a particularly appropriate object of study. In this study, the relationship between the price a man spent on the engagement ring and the appreciation of the gift by the partner receiving the gift is examined. Accordingly, newly engaged couples who either bought or received an engagement ring as a gift are interviewed on this issue. As a result, the study confirms on the one hand the assumption that engaged men as givers expect their fiancée to value the engagement ring more as the price increases. In contrast, however, no increase in appreciation with increasing price can be observed among women as recipients of the ring.

In the second study, participants in an online survey are asked in the role of givers and recipients to describe a gift they received or gave for birthday. At the same time, as givers, they are asked to indicate how much they paid for the gift and asked to rate how much the recipients are likely to have appreciated the gift. Respondents in the role of recipient are asked to estimate the price the giver probably spent on the gift they received and to name the degree of appreciation they felt. The results are similar to those from the first study: the givers see the price as a clear indicator of the expected appreciation of the recipient, while this connection between the price level and the appreciation of the gift cannot be proven among the recipients.

In the third study, the authors employ an experimental scenario in which they randomly assign participants the role of giver or receiver and place them in the hypothetical situation of giving or receiving either a small or a large (in the sense of: more expensive) gift. Thus, subjects have to put themselves in the assigned role and situation and indicate the degree of hypothetical pleasure they would experience as giver or receiver. Consistent with the other study results, it is also evident here that respondents in the giver role believe that the larger gift will be more enjoyable and appreciated than the smaller one, while respondents in the receiver role signal about the same degree of appreciation for both gifts.

Several **explanations** are offered for this **asymmetrical evaluation** of the connection between gift price and feelings of gratitude and joy, which are related to two phenomena already considered: the different evaluation situation in which giver and receiver find themselves, on the one hand, and the reciprocity rule, on the other.

Flynn and Adams (2009) point out that givers and receivers use **different modes of evaluation**. A giver will always consider multiple options in his or her deliberations, including assessing the effect of the gift on the recipient. When comparing two alternatives of different price or value, and thus often of different quality, it is only plausible that he or she will evaluate the more expensive, more valuable, and qualitatively superior option as a more promising gift. A recipient, on the other hand, has no options to evaluate, only the gift received. The only alternative is often not to receive a gift at all, which may already cause them to evaluate any gift positively in the first place. This argument considerably weakens the significance of the study results.

Irrespective of the studies presented, one reason for the asymmetrical valuation can be derived from the **reciprocity rule**, i.e. from the recipient's obligation to reciprocate and the associated unpleasant feeling of owing something to the giver. This aspect is also seen as a major reason for another phenomenon, namely that in some cases a high-priced gift does not trigger any enthusiasm or joy at all, but even reduces the satisfaction of the recipient and triggers rather ambivalent to negative feelings.

The acceptance of a gift is always connected with the recognition of a dependence, which can only be ended by a corresponding counter-gift. The more expensive the gift received is, the higher the tension felt by the recipients and the more annoying it is for them to spend a lot of money for the reduction of the tension, which they actually do not want to or cannot spend for this purpose. In this situation, they can not really enjoy the expensive gift.

But even in "unbalanced" relationships, in which the reciprocity rule is at least partially suspended, an expensive gift may be perceived as inappropriate by the recipient and even rejected. In direct line kinship relationships, for example, it is common for parents in financially superior situations to give larger gifts to their children who are students or in training. But here too, limits must be observed. If a gift reaches such a financial magnitude that it is understood by the children as a diffuse obligation for the future and a restriction of their freedom, it generates psychological and perhaps also real resistance. In the case of adult siblings, between whom it has long been clarified that income and asset relationships differ, a gift that is too expensive can cause discord. For even if there is agreement on both sides that financial reciprocity in exchange is neither necessary nor desirable, a very high-priced gift may be perceived not as generosity but as ostentatious evidence of superiority. It then appears as a manifestation of higher social status, and this does not lead to the cancellation of reciprocity. On the contrary: "when one person has higher status than another, it becomes acceptable to both parties for the bottom dog to contribute more" (Hochschild 2012, p. 84), be it in the form of demonstrations of gratitude, be it in the form of feelings of humiliation or guilt.

This already makes it clear that the consideration to which a recipient feels obliged does not always have to be money. In addition to emotional gratifications, it can also be, for example, support, help and accommodation. Belk and Coon (1993) examine the effect of **expensive gifts in dating relationships**. Here, it is not uncommon for men to extend expensive invitations, viewing them as an investment for which they expect something other than a return invitation of comparable financial value. Despite all the societal changes in role perceptions, the researchers still see the traditional dating roles in which men do the spending for the get-together while women balance the gift imbalance with affection, possibly also with sexual favors. An expensive dating gift, especially at the beginning of a relationship, seems to reveal the desired consideration and thus often generates less pleasure than resistance and psychological repulsion. Many female recipients gain the impression of being pressured, bought, or bribed by the giver. To get out of this uncomfortable emotional situation, some female recipients decide not to continue the dating relationship not despite but because of the expensive gift (Belk and Coon 1993; Marcoux 2009). In Margaret Mitchell's novel "Gone with the Wind," one episode makes abundantly clear the reciprocity considerations of Rhett Butler and Scarlett O'Hara in the giving and receiving of an expensive gift: the giver expresses his expectations of something in return, and the recipient – after brief resistance – considers a "very small" non-financial consideration to be acceptable.

> ### Margaret Mitchell: Gone with the Wind
>
> The beautiful Scarlett O'Hara, already widowed at the age of eighteen during the American Civil War, meets again the handsome, charming and self-confident Rhett Butler, whom she had met before, in Atlanta at a party for the benefit of the Southern Army. Rhett Butler makes an effort with the young widow, makes fun of her black mourning clothes, in which she would look like a crow and, moreover, ten years older, – and then presents his gift: a hatbox containing an expensive Parisian model hat. Scarlett is completely fascinated and cannot part with this hat, even though she knows that it is against all good manners for a lady to accept expensive gifts from a gentleman. Also, she is very aware that by accepting, it is to be expected that the giver would try to take liberties. Rhett Butler also leaves no doubt at all about his expectations of something in return: "Always remember I never do anything without reason and I never give anything without expecting something in return. I always get paid" (Mitchell 1964, p. 245).

4 The Financial Value of the Gift: Can't Buy Me... 57

Of course, this is an episode from a novel with a very specific place and time reference, since the action takes place in the southern states of the USA in 1861, the first year of the American Civil War. But the core message has not lost its relevance, even if donors in reality very rarely formulate their demand for payment for a generous gift so openly and directly.

The novel scene also makes clear another aspect that is a prerequisite for expensive gifts to trigger enthusiasm and joy: they must correspond exactly to the expressed or unexpressed wishes of the recipient. In the case of expressed wishes, this condition applies with regard to the type of gift as well as to the variant chosen. If the wife flirts with an expensive handbag but receives a necklace that is perhaps even more expensive, the gift is usually just as unsuccessful as in the case where the husband chooses the wrong expensive handbag. The exact execution of the specified gift task fills the recipient with relief and satisfaction, but rarely with enthusiasm. This, however, occurs when the secret – the not openly expressed and hardly signalled – wishes are directed precisely at this expensive product, but the recipient would never have dared to express this wish because, in view of conscious financial limits, it appeared to him to be unrealisable, and in any case immodest. In these cases, the enthusiasm results predominantly from the powerful symbols of the expensive gift. It is the great joy of guessing, even knowing, the secret desire, the surprise of receiving something longed for unexpectedly, and possibly also the emotional touch due to the knowledge of the sacrifice the giver is making with the gift. In Scarlett's case, several things come together: the great appreciation of the extremely expensive gift and, at the same time, the surprise and joy of receiving with the Paris hat something that she had not even secretly wished for, but of which she only knows and feels when she receives it that the gift exceeds anything she could possibly wish for.

A high financial value of a gift can therefore lead to the desired result, but it can by no means be assumed that the appreciation of the recipient always increases with the price. An expensive gift does not necessarily act as a persuasive proof of love. Consequently, the conclusion of Flynn and Adams (2009, p. 508) is: "Instead, it seems that money can't buy love and givers would do well to buy a thoughtful gift, rather than a more expensive one".

References

Belk RW, Coon GS (1993) Gift giving as agapic love: an alternative to the exchange paradigm based on dating experiences. J Consum Res 20(3):393–417

Camerer C (1988) Gifts as economic signals and social symbols. Am J Sociol 94(Supplement: Organizations and institutions: Sociological and economic approaches to the analysis of social structure):180–214

Flynn FJ, Adams GS (2009) Money can't buy love: asymmetric beliefs about gift price and feelings of appreciation. J Exp Soc Psychol 45(2):404–409

Hochschild AR (2012) The managed heart. Commercialization of human feeling. University of California Press, Berkeley

Larsen D, Watson JJ (2001) A guide map to the terrain of gift value. Psychol Mark 18(8):889–906

Marcoux J-S (2009) Escaping the gift economy. J Consum Res 36(4):671–685

Mitchell M (1964) Gone with the wind. Macmillan Publishing, New York

5

The Emotional Value of the Gift: Empathy, Surprise, Sacrifice

An economic view focuses on the objective value of a gift, the price, and thus, from the giver's point of view, the financial costs that he or she has to bear. However, it is known that the emotional value of the gift is usually of greater importance to the recipient. This also brings other cost categories of the giver into view for economists. They then speak of 'behavioural costs' with physical, psychic and temporal cost components (Robben and Verhallen 1994). But such economic labelling can well be dispensed with if we turn to the question of how emotional value is created. For the mechanisms of individualisation and symbolic charging responsible for this can be clearly identified. Most important are the empathy and good intentions of the giver, the surprise, and the sacrifices made and efforts taken in procuring and personally creating the gift. All these aspects lead to positive emotions in the recipient, which is the real purpose of a gift (Ruffle 1999).

Empathy is demonstrated by the fact that the gift is not based on the ideas of the giver, but is individually selected with regard to the person of the recipient. This includes that it is precisely tailored to the interests and wishes of the recipient, takes into account his or her current situation and state of mind, and also appears appropriate with regard to the status of the relationship.

As a yardstick for assessing the presence and strength of empathy, recipients do not only, and often not even primarily, take the gift itself. More decisive for their assessment are often the extent and intensity of the thoughts that the giver has put into the preparation phase in order to find and select the right gift. The corresponding thesis is: "It is the thought that counts" (Belk 1976; Moreau et al. 2011; Zhang and Epley 2012). This thesis is consistent with research findings on a related topic, namely the evaluation of help received (Ames et al. 2004). These show that only help that is given from the heart and based on genuine affection is truly appreciated by the recipient and positively influences his or her subsequent behaviour, in contrast to help that is given only because of obligatory role prescriptions or cost-benefit considerations. With reference to gift-giving, this means that a recipient perceives high value in a gift and positive feelings only if he is convinced that it was given out of genuine affection and not out of obligation or in view of a hoped-for consideration. In this sense, Ruth (1996, p. 211) extends or concretizes the 'intention thesis': "It is not only 'the thought that counts' but also the feelings".

Of course, this is also known to most givers, and therefore they try to express in the gift their thoughts and the perceived closeness of the relationship. However, difficulties sometimes arise in this process. On the one hand, **conflicts of motives** can arise in the preparation phase, and on the other hand, the recipient must also recognize the effort of thought in the exchange phase.

When choosing a gift, givers are sometimes faced with the question of whether to comply with an explicit wish of the recipient or to choose an alternative that they select specifically for the recipient. Two different motives come into competition. On the one hand, they want to fulfill the **wishes of the relationship partner**, but on the other hand, they also want to signal the **special closeness of the relationship** (Ward and Broniarczyk 2016). This situation arises in particular with the existence of wish lists, which are deposited with household stores and toy shops for various occasions such as weddings, children's birthdays or anniversaries, or are available on their homepages or special online sites. With a wish list, recipients can avoid unwanted and duplicate gifts, and givers are on the safe side as they cannot give the wrong gifts (Bradford and Sherry 2013). However, a wish list also limits the giver's freedom of choice. In the Chap. 1, this aspect has already been considered, in terms of the specific problem of donors having to give a gift that contradicts their self-image and identity due to the given alternatives. Here we are concerned with a different kind of restricted freedom of choice: in choosing an object from the catalogue of wishes, the givers are deprived of the possibility of expressing their special relationship with the recipient through a freely and individually chosen gift. This gives rise to the fear that the recipient might interpret the decision negatively, for example in the sense that the giver did not put enough thought and effort into finding a good gift for him.

In their study, Ward and Broniarczyk (2016) examine how donors behave in this conflict of motives. They find that, with regard to close friends, givers tend to ignore the explicit preferences of the recipients on the wish lists. They are dominated by a stronger desire to use their gift choice as a relationship signal; they want to adequately demonstrate friendship closeness and receive appropriate recognition. Gifts that are easily procured, widely available, or suggested by recipients do not provide an opportunity for this.

Psychologically, givers often resolve the conflicting goals of their motives through a cognitive adjustment process. They perceive the gift options in a distorted way and come to believe that the freely chosen gift with relationship signals fits the preferences of the recipient better than a gift from the wish list. Since this need not correspond to reality, the free choice of unregistered gifts is a risky strategy with a reduced probability that the gifts will please the recipients.

Towards less close friends, the acquaintances at a greater emotional distance, the situation looks different. Here, giving is more of a social obligation, the gifts communicate fewer feelings and are symbolically charged to a lesser extent. Therefore, in these cases, givers do not feel the motivational conflict as strongly, are less susceptible to perceptual distortions of gift options, and are more likely to select something from the wish list. This leads, as the authors say, 'ironically' to the consequence that givers are more likely to select successful gifts for their more distant acquaintances, while their concern to provide a relationship signal for their good friends prevents them from giving them a gift that matches their preferences (Ward and Broniarczyk 2016, p. 1002).

The fact that gifts chosen with good intentions are not always the optimal choice also seems to be confirmed by other studies. For example, in the experiments conducted by Gino and Flynn (2011), participants believed in their role as givers that gifts selected from a wish list would be valued less by the recipient than gifts they had not specifically requested. But the results of the study clearly contradicted this assumption. Respondents in the recipient role valued the receipt of a solicited gift more than a non-desired but thoughtful gift.

Such research results are worth considering and informative. However, they do not constitute proof that recipients in every case actually rate a freely chosen and considered gift, especially from a friend, with which the latter expresses the particularly close relationship, worse than a gift from the wish list. On the one hand, it depends on the respective gifts to be compared; on the other hand, it is precisely the recognisable effort to do justice to the specific, personal relationship in the gift that can be of high symbolic significance and thus have a superior emotional value from the recipient's point of view.

Results of a study by Givi and Galak (2017) can also be interpreted in this direction. They study the case where givers are faced with the choice of gifts with different emotional value. On the one hand, they may choose a gift that exactly matches the preferences and tastes of the recipient: a new book by the favorite author, a fan item from the favorite soccer team, or favorite flowers, i.e., a kind of gift they can't go wrong with. On the other hand, these are gifts that have a higher emotional value, for example because they contain a positive memory of an important event or a shared experience, such as a photo or a souvenir of a trip. They also include gifts with a higher degree of surprise and a greater investment of time and effort. In the study, it appears that recipients often opt for the more emotionally valuable gifts, but givers prefer to choose gifts in the first category. This asymmetry can be explained by the different degree of certainty or uncertainty associated with the gifts. As a rule, givers can be largely certain that gifts that exactly match the recipient's preferences will be well received by the recipient, whereas with the more emotionally valuable gifts they feel uncertainty about the effect on the recipient and therefore shy away from the choice. In this case, this means that a well-considered emotionally superior variant is not chosen because the giver is uncertain whether his well-intentioned considerations and intentions will also be recognized and appreciated.

This result implicitly points to the second problem mentioned, which can occur if one relies on the validity of the thesis "It is the thought that counts": it is not certain that the recipient will **perceive** the good thoughts.

Everyday experience and empirical studies show that recipients by no means always reflect and correctly assess the intentions and thoughts of the recipient. Apparently, a special trigger is required for recipients to be prompted to think for themselves about the thoughts of the giver. If they objectively like a gift, they usually do not perceive the thoughtful effort of the giver, or even if they do, this does not increase their appreciation and gratitude. This is because in such situations, the objective quality of the gift, which is immediately visible and can be evaluated, is of primary importance, but the invisible thoughts of the giver are of secondary relevance (Zhang and Epley 2012; Galak et al. 2016).

But what causes a recipient to reflect the donor's considerations? Two things play a decisive role here. Firstly, the violation of expectations, and secondly, direct indications from the giver.

If the perception of a gift received differs massively from the recipient's clear or even diffuse expectations, **cognitive processes** are immediately triggered to provide an explanation for this discrepancy. In the case of a **positive discrepancy**, this means that the recipient's expectations of the donor's mental effort have been significantly exceeded. This may be due to the donor having given relatively thoughtless gifts in the past. Similarly, it is conceivable that the amount of thought required for the current gift far exceeds the usual or previously experienced level. A friend's gift, which deviated from a wish list but was very successful, may also be such a thought trigger.

A significant **negative discrepancy** also leads to cognitive processes and adjustments. If a close friend or family member comes with a gift that the recipient considers exceptionally inappropriate, they will also wonder why. Then the interpretation can go in two directions. On the one hand, it is possible that what is received is seen as a signal of a low level of mental investment in the relationship on the part of the giver, which is accompanied by corresponding negative feelings. On the other hand, the recipient may also discover in his or her mental preoccupation with the gift the good intention of the giver that was the cause of the choice, the positive evaluation of which then reduces or compensates for the spontaneous disappointment.

If donors have doubts as to whether their own mental effort is perceived, it seems sensible to **communicate** this **openly**. They will then explain in the accompanying words during the handover what considerations they have made and what intention they are pursuing. In this way, they can ensure that their good intention is appreciated in terms of a positive increase in value.

However, since not every gift can be provided with an explanation and not all givers want to put themselves in a special light, the authors recommend not necessarily trusting that one's own thoughtful effort will be recognised by the recipient, and not being disappointed if this is not actually the case. When in doubt, they should rather opt for gifts with which less thought is involved but which have a **high objective value**: "If you want to give a gift that someone will appreciate, then you should focus on getting a good gift and ignore whether it is a thoughtful gift or not" (Zhang and Epley 2012, p. 679). With this recommendation, however, one should not overlook the introductory condition "in doubt". This is because, in most cases, recipients have a keen sense of the thoughtful effort involved in a gift and value it highly accordingly. In this respect, it seems sensible to continue to assume the validity of the 'intention thesis' and to deviate from it only in exceptional cases.

Besides or together with empathy, it is **surprise** that can trigger spontaneous joy, even enthusiasm, in the recipient. No wonder that surprise is one of the qualities that characterize a perfect gift according to Belk (1996). Surprise is usually already present when one receives a gift seemingly without any occasion and without any prospect of receiving anything in return. In most cases, however, people give each other something for a specific occasion: a birthday, an engagement, Valentine's Day, Mother's Day, or Christmas. And everyone involved is aware that gifts are being presented. Therefore, it is not the fact that one receives a gift that is surprising, but which gift one receives (Schwaiger 2011, p. 135).

A surprising gift is one that one did not expect at all. Therefore, this new situation, with which one is confronted unprepared, triggers intense cognitive and emotional reactions. These reactions are of course positive in the case that one receives much more or something much better than one had hoped for or even something one had hardly dared to hope for. These positive reactions are usually what a giver's intentions are aimed at. Imagining how the surprised recipient will react in amazement and excitement with facial expressions, body language and words is part of their anticipation. Therefore, part of gift giving is subtly exploring the recipient's desires. Equally important are secrecy about the decision, hiding, and sometimes even sending signals that lead the recipient down the wrong thought paths, such as when givers pretend not to have a gift idea or respond with ostensible disinterest to expressed cues (Clarke 2006). And if the surprise is successful and the hoped-for reaction actually occurs during the exchange, the giver feels pride and joy at the success of his or her plan (Ruffle 1999).

Of course, surprises can also go wrong. In this respect, there are sometimes unpleasant surprises, for example when a gift unexpectedly appears to be completely inappropriate, inadaquate for the occasion, tasteless or cheap. But also a gift that is too big, too expensive can be an "overkill", an unpleasant surprise because it does not correspond to the state of the relationship (Ruth et al. 1999, p. 393). Problems can also arise if the recipients have explicitly expressed a particular wish in advance or have given supposedly clear signs that they assume will certainly not be overlooked and correctly decoded (Galak et al. 2016). Those who unexpectedly discover when unwrapping the gift that they do not receive what they wanted experience a nasty surprise that immediately triggers negative emotions such as disappointment and dissatisfaction; emotions that are also expressed in facial expressions and body language and are therefore difficult to conceal.

This should be borne in mind when asking a person to be given a gift directly about his or her wishes or receiving from him or her a wish list – possibly with a precise indication of priorities. If one fulfils the request, one cannot really surprise; and a possibly feigned surprise by the recipient is implausible (Ruffle 1999). However, if one does not fulfill the request, one surprises the recipient negatively, which may cause frustration instead of joy. This is especially important to keep in mind with regard to gifts for children. While many adults often appear to be wish-less or satisfy their needs immediately, it is different for children. They want something very special for their birthday or for Christmas. Before Christmas, they write and design wish lists with imagination, anticipation and hope, and often with very clear ideas. An Austrian analysis of wish list letters to the Christ Child shows, for example, that a significant proportion has the character of shopping or order lists, not infrequently including brand names (Waiguny et al. 2012). In an earlier American analysis of letters to Santa Claus, over 80% of children mention at least one brand name (Otnes et al. 1994). Surprise, in the sense of deviation from the desired, is completely misplaced here. If children do not get what is hotly desired, or even something undesirable, on such occasions, which are associated with particularly high expectations, this can only be understood by them as an expression of their parents' lack of love and their ignorance of their wishes (Belk 1996). Nevertheless, the situation is not always easy, because not every wish for a child can be fulfilled for financial reasons alone, and children also tend to have quite a few and sometimes changing very greatest wishes. Such a situation requires clear communication between the parents at an early stage in order to bring the children's expectations to a realistic level and to avoid disappointment (Otnes et al. 1994).

The actual fulfillment of a heart's desire creates enthusiasm, which is only increased when the gift is in a form that exceeds all children's dreams. Surprises through further gifts increase the joy, but are not decisive. This is also how the boy Hanno experiences the giving of presents on Christmas Eve in the Buddenbrook house, depicted in what is surely the most famous chapter of Thomas Mann's novel of the decline of a family, which was awarded the Nobel Prize for Literature in 1929.

> **Thomas Mann: Buddenbrooks**
>
> Despite economic and personal crises, the Buddenbrook house does not cut back on its brilliantly celebrated Christmas. The consul oversees the solemn traditional program. Only two children are present. One is Hanno, Consul Thomas' only son and thus the last heir, who, a tender child with musical interests, to his father's disappointment lacks any incli-

5 The Emotional Value of the Gift: Empathy... 69

> nation or aptitude for what should have been a merchant's profession. And Hanno waits with a pounding heart for the presents. His most ardent wish is a puppet theater. As compensation and reward for a visit to the dentist, he had been allowed to visit the municipal theatre for the first time with his mother and attend a performance of 'Fidelio'. Since then, he has been dreaming of the puppet theater and imagining the details, such as what size it would be, what the curtain would look like, and whether the decorations for Fidelio would also be there. And when, after the reading of the Christmas story and the singing of Christmas carols, the high double door is finally opened, his feverishly searching eyes immediately find the hoped-for puppet theater. Although his grandmother first leads him to a special gift, a harmonium, also the fulfillment of an "overpowering" dream, all his interest, and all his attention, is directed to the puppet theater, on whose stage the decoration of the last act of Fidelio is set up. Hanno is overjoyed.
>
> The harmonium was the surprise, very beautiful, even overpowering, but what would have been if the puppet theater had been missing? (Mann 1993, p. 466).

In addition to empathy and surprise, it is the **effort and sacrifice** that a giver makes for a gift that constitutes the emotional value of a gift. For example, if someone takes action in a variety of ways, overcomes great difficulties and spends a great deal of time, for example, to acquire a desired book antiquarian or to find a missing specimen of a coin collection, then he or she can usually expect that the recipient will reward this special effort with joy and gratitude. The same is true if the gift involves a significant sacrifice on the part of the giver. This can be of a financial nature if, for example, a gift only becomes affordable for someone by foregoing the fulfilment of the own needs and wishes or possibly even taking out a loan which subsequently has to be paid off for a long time to come. But the sacrifice can also consist in the givers' parting with own gifts that have a high symbolic value for themselves. A woman who gives her own mother's special jewellery to her daughter-in-law on the occasion of her son's wedding will certainly not give up this valuable memento lightly. But if she does, it is in the hope that the daughter-in-law will appreciate the sacrifice associated with the gift. However, the basic prerequisite here is again the appropriate perception by the recipient. Only when the recipients recognize the commitment and sacrifice of the giver will the emotional value of the gift emerge and be appreciated accordingly.

The efforts of a giver are quite obvious if he has created the gift himself: self-sewn ties and knitted sweaters, a candle arch as a fretwork or self painted watercolors – such personally produced gifts demonstrate the use of skill and time, and in many cases recipients will appreciate this and perceive the emotional value. However, this only applies without restriction if it is children who are giving away their self-painted or hand-crafted products. Parents and grandparents are usually very happy about a picture that their (grand)daughter proudly presents to them. In the opposite case, a joyful reaction is hardly to be expected.

In the case of adults, own work is usually welcome if it involves **smaller gifts** that can be consumed – such as jams or gingerbread, candles or soaps. In the case of larger products that are visible in the long term, certain **conditions** must always be met to trigger joy. Above all, it is important to avoid letting the **preferences of the gift-giver** dominate and the perspective of the recipient go unnoticed. Just because someone knows how to paint quite well, the recipients do not necessarily enjoy paintings and share the painter's taste. Moreover, if they hang up the painting despite displeasure, they also increase the risk that such gifts will become the norm, so that they will look forward to the next occasion with concern rather than with joy.

The dominance of the giver's perspective is also present when the gift primarily serves the purpose of

self-presentation. Those who use a gift situation to present themselves as a particularly talented painter, singer or poet make it clear to all present that for them the recipient is not in the foreground. This is for them only cause for narcissistic self-congratulation, and even a successful appearance fails as a gift. Also, the object must at least be of such high **quality** that joy can be shown at the reception without hypocrisy. A self-knitted cap with holes in the stitch pattern or a bird house glued together crookedly are annoying not only on receipt, but also later when they are seen. That's why they usually end up in the dustbin and – if little consideration is given – in the garbage can.

A particularly impressive example of lifelong unforgettable annoyance due to self-made gifts is provided by Thomas Bernhard in a short scene from his novel "Auslöschung – ein Zerfall" ("Extinction").

> **Thomas Bernhard: Extinction**
>
> In this autobiographically influenced novel, the protagonist Franz-Josef Murau settles accounts with his home in Wolfsegg, Upper Austria. He hates everything, the National Socialist-Catholic environment, his parents, his brother and his sisters, who terrorize all family members with their homemade knitting at Christmas. According to his description, the whole pre-Christmas period is already dominated by wool and sweater knitting, but it is worst on Christmas Eve after the gift-giving. Everyone sits around in the ugly, ill-fitting and scatchy sweaters, feeling as if they've been mutilated. And the most annoying is that the tortured recipients also have to thank the givers for it (Bernhard 2011).

It can thus be noted that donors can give high emotional value to their gifts with empathy, surprises and the commitment of effort and sacrifice. However, this value is not an objective quantity, but exists only in the perception of the recipient. Therefore, it is important for givers to ensure that their thoughts and considerations, their physical, time and financial efforts, and their sacrifices are recognized by the recipient. It is also important to avoid negative surprises and to ensure that their gift is truly about the recipient and not about themselves.

References

Ames DR et al (2004) It's the thought that counts: on perceiving how helpers decide to lend a hand. Personal Soc Psychol Bull 30(4):461–474

Belk RW (1976) It's the thought that counts: a signed digraph analysis of gift-giving. J Consum Res 3(3):155–162

Belk RW (1996) The perfect gift. In: Otnes C, Beltramini RF (eds) Gift giving: a research anthology. Bowling Green State University Popular Press, Bowling Green, pp 59–85

Bernhard T (2011) Extinction: a novel. Vintage Books, New York

Bradford TW, Sherry JF (2013) Orchestrating rituals through retailers: an examination of gift registry. J Retail 89(2):158–175

Clarke P (2006) Christmas gift giving involvement. J Consum Mark 23(5):283–291

Galak J et al (2016) Why certain gifts are great to give but not to get: a framework for understanding errors in gift giving. Curr Dir Psychol Sci 25(6):380–385

Gino F, Flynn F (2011) Give them what they want: the benefits of explicitness in gift exchange. Adv Consum Res 38:198–199

Givi J, Galak J (2017) Sentimental value and gift giving: givers' fears of getting it wrong prevents them from getting it right. J Consum Psychol 27(4):473–479

Mann T (1993) Buddenbrooks. The decline of a family. Alfred A. Knopf, New York

Moreau CP et al (2011) It's the thought (and the effort) that counts: how customizing for others differs from customizing for oneself. J Mark 75(5):120–133

Otnes C et al (1994) All I want for Christmas: an analysis of children's brand requests to Santa Claus. J Pop Cult 27(4):183–194

Robben HSJ, Verhallen TMM (1994) Behavioral costs as determinants of cost perception and preference formation for gifts to receive and gifts to give. J Econ Psychol 15(2):333–350

Ruffle BJ (1999) Gift giving with emotions. J Econ Behav Organ 39(4):399–420

Ruth JA (1996) It's the feeling that counts: toward an understanding of emotion and its influence on the gift-exchange processes. In: Otnes C, Beltramini RF (eds) Gift giving: a research anthology. Bowling Green State University Press, Bowling Green, pp 195–214

Ruth JA et al (1999) Gift receipt and the reformulation of interpersonal relationships. J Consum Res 25(4):385–402

Schwaiger H (2011) Schenken. Entwurf einer sozialen Morphologie aus Perspektive der Kommunikationstheorie. UVK Verlag, Konstanz

Waiguny MKJ et al (2012) When Xmas wishes are brands: wishing behavior of children. In: Eisend M et al (eds) Advances in advertising research, vol III, Wiesbaden, pp 303–319

Ward MK, Broniarczyk SM (2016) Ask and you shall (not) receive: close friends prioritize relational signaling over recipient preferences in their gift choices. J Mark Res 53(6):1001–1018

Zhang Y, Epley N (2012) Exaggerated, mispredicted, and misplaced: when "it's the thought that counts" in gift exchanges. J Exp Psychol Gen 141(4):667–681

6

Gifts as Information Media: What They Say About the Giver and the Relationship with the Recipient

In considering the emotional value of gifts, it has already become clear what scientific research from several disciplines – ethnography, psychology, and sociology – has consistently emphasized: gifts are significant **means of social communication**. They are a kind of **symbolic language** used to make important statements about interpersonal relationships (Caplow 1984; Belk and Coon 1993; Ruth 1996). We learned this language of gift-giving in childhood, although it is not practiced in any kindergarten learning game and is not on any school curriculum. We master the language throughout our lives, even without always being aware of it. We cannot unlearn it or choose to forget it, just as we cannot forget our mother tongue. With every gift we receive, we receive messages; with every gift we give, especially to those who are close to us, we must be careful not to send unpleasant or hostile messages through carelessness.

There are **two sensitive facts** in particular about which gifts contain information: on the one hand, about the

person of the giver, on the other hand, about how the giver sees the recipient and – linked to this – about the **state of the relationship** between the exchange partners.

First of all, gifts say a lot about the givers, their character and qualities. This can be intentional if the givers want to convey a certain image of themselves with the gift, if they want to show who they are, how they are or how they would like to be seen (Belk 1979; Wooten 2000). But a gift also contains a message about the giver independent of any intentional staging. This is because the recipients spontaneously read off the amount of financial and emotional investment from the gift. They thus perceive whether the givers are generous or stingy, whether they think primarily egoistically of themselves and their advantage or of the recipient, whether they are concerned with them and take trouble for them or not. Gifts thus reveal the givers in terms of their ego, their properties, the degree of empathy, love, commitment and generosity characteristic of them (Belk and Coon 1993). They also give clear indications of the givers' interests, preferences, competencies and tastes. A gift is thus to a great extent a self-expression by the givers, who transfer a part of themselves to the receiver, thus revealing much of themselves – in line with the motto "Show me what you give and I will tell you who you are". The German writer Joachim Ringelnatz sums up this situation in his poem "Schenken" ('Gift-giving') with the final recommendation to the giver: 'Be mindful that your gift is yourself' (Ringelnatz 1994, p. 265).

Gifts not only contain important information about the givers, but also about how the **givers see their role in the relationship**, and thus at the same time what role they assign to the recipient. Otnes et al. (1993) show in their study that gift givers can assume six different social roles towards the recipients: pleaser, provider, socializer, compensator, acknowledger and avoider.

Pleasers choose gifts that they think the recipient will like. They care a lot about proving to the recipient how much they value him or her and how much they care about the relationship. Therefore, they buy things that are explicitly desired by the recipient or that they are sure, through observation and indirect evidence, will meet the recipient's desires. And they buy the corresponding object even in the case that the gifts do not correspond to their own taste. Things made by oneself are also given away, but only in the definite knowledge that these gifts are really wanted. And knowing the special interests and wishes, they also set out to find a 'treasure' that is of special significance only to the recipient. In any case, the message of the gift is "I want to give you the greatest possible pleasure".

Providers typically give useful gifts that they assume the recipients lack but do not necessarily want. Mostly, the gifts are utilitarian items. Providers usually get the gifts in advance, so they buy Christmas gifts throughout the year, for example, and have a specific place – like a compartment in the closet – to store the gifts. They also often care about giving lots of gifts to express their caring for the recipient in quantitative terms. Thus, the message of their gifts is "I care about your needs".

Compensators strive to use their gift to help the recipient cope with a loss he or she is experiencing or has experienced. It is a kind of consolation in difficult times, for example in the phase after the loss of a family member or even after a financial loss. Other occasions can be psychologically and physically painful events such as a divorce, the children moving away or an accident. The role of the compensator has elements of pleaser and provider. In this respect, the compensator also adopts the gift strategies observed in these two roles. However, the message is specific: "I share in your difficult situation and would like to give you some relief".

Socializers use gifts as a tool to educate and impart new values or knowledge to the recipient, even though these gifts may not be desired. The primary goal here is not to please the recipients, but to guide and develop them in a certain direction. Often such gifts are chosen by parents for their children, but not as a sole strategy, but in combination with another role, especially that of the pleaser, in order not to produce disappointment. Nevertheless, the dominant message remains "I know what is good for you".

Acknwoledger recognize (by necessity) the fact that there is a relationship that requires a gift. So they only give gifts because they feel this is obligatory. This is especially true towards people who are more on the fringes of the social network, who live far away and with whom there is little experience of exchanging gifts. In an analogous way, the role of the acknowleder is taken in the case of close relatives, when the relationship is clouded and fraught with tension. Here, the recipients are primarily seen as difficult and appropriate strategies are chosen, which will be discussed in Chap. 9. The mostly uncreative and hardly individualized gifts of the acknowledgers communicate: "Here comes my gift, because it is just common".

Avoiders seek to prevent or minimize relationship building by refusing to engage in the exchange of gifts. This refusal is associated with a dismissive message that can vary in severity. It ranges from "I am not interested in a closer relationship with you" to "You are not worthy of receiving a gift in general or at this time."

Of course, individual givers may also play different roles towards different recipients, a phenomenon for which the authors choose the metaphor "chameleon" (Otnes et al. 1993, p. 232). This is because large gift-giving occasions such as Christmas involve many members of a social network, and these relationships can vary greatly. Recipients with whom there is a very close or a very loose relationship, or a very positive, indifferent or negative relationship, must receive a gift simultaneously, resulting in givers varying their role in each case depending on the nature of the relationship.

Gifts thus inform the **recipients** which of these roles the giver assumes and which role is thus assigned to them, and the recipients evaluate this understanding of the role. Of course, the role of the avoider has a negative connotation, since the givers clearly signal that they are seeking to weaken or dissolve the relationship. The role of the acknowledgers, who only give because they feel obliged, is also perceived rather negatively. In contrast, the assessment of the pleasers, who are oriented towards the wishes of the recipient, is fundamentally positive. However, positive intention is not enough. Givers must also prove their detailed knowledge of the recipient, because ignorance also has a symbolic character. For example, clothing in the wrong size is one of the most disappointing standard gifts. Women feel particularly critical when they receive oversized garments, which appears as evidence that the giver thinks they are fatter than they are. Similarly, children and adolescents feel offended when they receive toys or accessories that signal that they are judged to be too young and small (Caplow 1984). The role of compensator is also perceived in a rather appreciative way, as the good intention of helping and comforting is valued positively.

The situation is more ambivalent in the other roles. When the giver takes on the roles of socialiser and provider, good intentions are also present, but the giver perspective dominates. Problems can arise from this when recipients feel that their interests or tastes are not adequately respected or that they are being controlled. For example, teenage daughters often reject gifts of clothing from their mothers, not only because they see them as inappropriate or unfortunate, but because they want to gain autonomy over their clothing choices (Corrigan 1989). And this role conflict extends far beyond the teenage phase. For example, a study by Liu et al. (2019) shows that even adult daughters resist gifts from their socializing mothers intended to educate or morally guide them. Conversely, older mothers resist their daughters' socializing efforts when the daughters give objectively useful products that make life easier in old age, but the mothers view their use as an intrusion into their best practices and lifestyles and reject them.

Similar problems can arise when taking on the role of provider. Providers do orient themselves to the needs of the recipient – or better: to the recipient's objective needs – but this is only a successful strategy if the recipient's wishes go in this direction. If parents give their children thoroughly useful gifts, but these are interpreted by the children as renewed evidence of parental disregard and disrespect for their intellectual interests or artistic ambitions, the relationship is impaired.

The information about the giver's understanding of what he or she and the exchange partner perceive is already communicating important statements about the **state of the relationship** from the giver's point of view. But recipients understand a wealth of other aspects of giving and perceived financial and emotional investment as statements about the nature and intensity of the relationship.

Characteristics of gifts such as quality and price, the extent of thoughtful consideration and empathy, time and effort in preliminary deliberations, selection strategies, and procurement, all provide information about the closeness and warmth of a relationship (Otnes et al. 1993; Joy 2001). Where the relationship grows cold, investment declines, and declining investment in the relationship in turn signals that the relationship is losing intensity. Unkind gifts illustrate that unkindness is present in a relationship. In this respect, gifts are considered important indicators of relationship strength and quality (Ruth et al. 1999; Schwaiger 2011), indeed they virtually symbolize the relationship (Sherry 1983).

Gifts that contain messages of perceived similarity and shared good memories have a particularly positive and relationship-strengthening effect.

The extent to which partners perceive each other as **similar** is a decisive factor for satisfaction in the relationship and its stability in all its phases. Therefore, gifts are also considered an essential indication of interpersonal similarity in terms of interests and tastes, and thus of the compatibility of the parties involved (Belk and Coon 1993; Larsen and Watson 2001; Dunn et al. 2008). This is especially true for partner relationships. Here, gifts have great symbolic power by showing whether one is a good match for the other. 'Inappropriate' gifts reduce perceived similarity and are likely to weaken the relationship, whereas 'appropriate' gifts increase perceptions of similarity and are relationship strengthening (Caplow 1984; Dunn et al. 2008).

Similarity is especially evident in the fact that partners are passionate about the **same things**, such as art, literature or travel. Similar interests make it easier to give suitable gifts. It is known from studies that predictions about which products their partners would like are primarily determined by their own product preferences (Davis et al. 1986). Accordingly, people who are similar to their gift partner may also make better predictions, i.e., make more correct gift decisions. At the same time, similarity of interest also creates opportunities for exchange about the gift, possibly an opportunity for sharing, for example, attending a concert or taking a cruise resulting in shared memories. Equally positive things can be said about similarities in taste. As has been known since the work of the French sociologist Bourdieu (2010), differences in taste are not only to be understood as individual inclinations, but above all as the outflow of different milieu-specific imprints. Therefore, these taste 'subtle differences' have a particularly divisive effect, while commonalities in taste signal belonging. Accordingly, gifts with identical tastes reinforce this signal.

While the previous review focused on the similarity of gift partners, other researchers examine the effect of the similarity of a material gift to objects in the giver's own possession. Polman and Maglio (2017) examine this phenomenon, although the concept of similarity they choose does not quite accurately capture the issue. Namely, they explore the question of whether it has a positive effect on the recipient's appreciation of a gift if recipients know that the giver owns or has also purchased the identical object for themselves. In fact, they find a "companionizing effect". According to this, recipients value a gift more simply because they know that the object received 'accompanies' an identical object owned by the giver. According to the researchers, this effect is not due to the fact that the recipient sees the fact of the same possession as an indicator of better quality, increased effort or pre-existing closeness in the relationship. The accompaniment effect is explained by the fact that people who have something in common develop a sense of connection. This applies to a wide variety of aspects such as having the same first name or the same birthday – and equally to material things. The fact that the givers have also acquired the same object for themselves connects and reminds the recipients of the givers when they use it. In this respect, it seems to make sense for givers to point out that it is a 'companion gift' when handing it over.

Especially positive emotions and thoughts are triggered by gifts whose messages consist in the revival of happily **experienced moments together**. These are gifts such as the catalogue of an exhibition visited, a coffee-table book of a recent travel destination, a souvenir from the museum shop. They all have lasting value because they recall a moment of particularly close connection and shared experience. Self-created photo books represent this type of gift particularly impressively. They capture all the good moments of recent times, the wonderful days spent together, impressions of trips, family celebrations, visits to the zoo and amusement park with the grandchildren. Each opening of such a book activates the positive experiences at that time, provides an opportunity to remember together the occasions and the details already faded in memory (clothes, sights, weather, incidents). Therefore, such gifts not only give pleasure when received, but are usually kept for a long time as symbols of emotional attachment, because they activate earlier positive experiences and emotions, 'create a kind of memory' (Schwaiger 2011, p. 118) and deepen the felt commonality with the memory.

Gifts therefore communicate a great deal of information about the giver, the giver's view of the recipient and the state of the relationship. In this respect, it is necessary to consider already in the preparation phase which messages one would like to send or how recipients could decode any messages. A wrong word can usually be taken back, a wrong gift hardly.

References

Belk RW (1979) Gift giving behavior. In: Sheth JN (ed) Research in marketing, Bd 2. JAI Press, Greenwich, pp 95–126

Belk RW, Coon GS (1993) Gift giving as agapic love: an alternative to the exchange paradigm based on dating experiences. J Consum Res 20(3):393–417

Bourdieu P (2010) Distinction: a social critique of the judgement of taste. Routledge, London

Caplow T (1984) Rule enforcement without visible means: Christmas gift giving in Middletown. Am J Soc 89(6):1306–1323

Corrigan P (1989) Gender and the gift: the case of the family clothing economy. Sociology 23(4):513–534

Davis HL et al (1986) An anchoring and adjustment model of spousal predictions. J Consum Res 13(1):25–37

Dunn EW et al (2008) The gift of similarity: how good and bad gifts influence relationships. Soc Cogn 26(4):469–481

Joy A (2001) Gift giving in Hong Kong and the continuum of social ties. J Consum Res 28(2):239–256

Larsen D, Watson JJ (2001) A guide map to the terrain of gift value. Psychol Mark 18(8):889–906

Liu C et al (2019) Gift-giving within adult daughter-mother dyads. In: Minowa Y, Belk RW (eds) Gifts, romance, and consumer culture. Routledge, New York, pp 141–152

Otnes C et al (1993) Gift selection for easy and difficult recipients: a social roles interpretation. J Consum Res 20(2):229–244

Polman E, Maglio SJ (2017) Mere gifting: liking a gift more because it is shared. Personal Soc Psychol Bull 43(11):1582–1194

Ringelnatz J (1994) Schenken. In: Ringelnatz J (ed) Das Gesamtwerk in sieben Bänden, vol 1, Gedichte 1. Diogenes Verlag, Zürich

Ruth JA (1996) It's the feeling that counts: toward an understanding of emotion and its influence on the gift-exchange processes. In: Otnes C, Beltramini RF (eds) Gift giving: a research anthology. Bowling Green State University Press, Bowling Green, pp 195–214

Ruth JA et al (1999) Gift receipt and the reformulation of interpersonal relationships. J Consum Res 25(4):385–402

Schwaiger H (2011) Schenken. Entwurf einer sozialen Morphologie aus Perspektive der Kommunikationstheorie. UVK Verlag, Konstanz

Sherry JF (1983) Gift giving in anthropological perspective. J Consum Res 10(2):157–168

Wooten DB (2000) Qualitative steps toward an expanded model of anxiety in gift-giving. J Consum Res 27(1):84–95

7

Gifts in Romantic Relationships: What Enhances and What Weakens the Relationship?

The emotional value of gifts and the messages contained in gifts about the givers, their view of the recipient, and the intensity of the emotional bond are especially significant in romantic relationships. This is because gift-giving is, throughout the world, a form of conveying romantic emotions, a great way of communicating intangible feelings of affection, intimacy and passion through a tangible object. This is done in the context of rituals such as Valentine's Day, rites of passage such as engagement and marriage, and even casual occasions that serve only to initiate, maintain, or strengthen the romantic relationship. Given this importance, it is not surprising that gift research has devoted particular attention to this area of application (Belk and Coon 1993; Otnes et al. 1994; Rugimbana et al. 2003; Saad and Gill 2003; Schiffman and Cohn 2009).

A romantic relationship is of a certain duration and is therefore different from a momentary falling in love or flirtation (Huang and Yu 2000). The main focus of gift-giving related research and analysis is on the early stage of a romantic relationship, which is characterized by unlimited passion for another person and is associated with intense feelings of attraction, fascination and idealization. At this stage of the relationship, gifts are virtually used as a "courtship tactic" (Nepomuceno et al. 2016, p. 27), and even small gifts such as a rose represent a romantic gesture that signals the desire for a more intense relationship.

But romantic love is not a constant, but changes over time, so that different phases with fluid transitions can be distinguished, from occasional meetings to regular dating, exclusive dating, living together, getting engaged and married until – in the lucky case – the period of long cohabitation follows. Here, let us only roughly distinguish between **two phases of romantic love**. One is the initial relationship building, characterized by passion with the aforementioned strong feelings ('beginning love' or 'dating'), and the other is love in long-term relationships, which is less erotically determined, more companionate in character, and helps partners stay together ('lasting love').

Beginning love has already been referred to by Belk (1996) when he developed his characterization of the perfect gift as an expression of selfless love using the example of a couple young in love. This ideal of gift-giving among couples (Minowa and Belk 2019, p. 38) corresponds to the paradigm of 'agapic' love, in which economic exchange considerations of reciprocity play no role, but rather altruistic donors give an expressive gift to a recipient whom they recognize and idealize in his or her uniqueness (Belk and Coon 1993).

Research on gifts in the phase of beginning love focuses on various questions. In particular, answers are sought to the questions of what special occasions there are for romantic gifts, what motives donors in romantic relationships pursue with their gifts, what requirements a perfect romantic gift must meet in order to trigger the desired emotions, and what types of gifts prove particularly suitable in romantic relationships.

In terms of **occasions**, **Valentine's Day** in particular has received special attention. This has its origins in medieval British customs, but has now become established almost worldwide as a commercial holiday to celebrate romantic love through gift-giving. Given its cultural embeddedness, Valentine's Day is not only highly symbolic but also of considerable economic importance (Rugimbana et al. 2003). In the United States, people planned to spend just under $22 billion on Valentine's Day gifts in 2021, an amount that is lower than the previous year ($27.4 billion) for the first time, presumably due to the Corona pandemic crisis (Statista 2021b).

Corporate marketing both demonstrates and promotes this importance. With an abundance of advertisements, TV commercials, online communication and displays or special areas in stores, it conveys the message weeks in advance that on this day, giving a gift to one's loved one is obligatory. Thus it fuels the expectations of having to give a gift, but also of receiving a gift. Thereby, the images of happy couples also shape the ideas of the feelings of closeness and togetherness to be experienced on the day, which are achieved through gifts. Men in particular are targeted as potential buyers, and are given gift and behavioural suggestions. In doing so, they are often given hints that go beyond traditional gifts such as flowers or sweets, such as using the day to make their sweetheart's day memorable with an engagement ring, which naturally raises expectations on the part of women as well. As a result, it also happens that the hoped for and desired positive feelings of love, affection and intimacy are not always triggered because expectations remain unfulfilled. One such case is a Valentine's Day experience described by a woman in the context of an empirical study.

Her boyfriend had invited her to a very extravagant picnic and presented her with a special Godiva chocolate box on this occasion. Given the circumstances, she had expected to find an engagement ring in the beautiful package. However, when the chocolate box actually contained only chocolate, she was disappointed, and the whole day was contaminated with it (Close and Zinkhan 2006, p. 363).

A survey on Valentine's Day 2020 makes clear which gifts men and women in Germany consider unsuitable or suitable for this occasion. Unsurprisingly, more than 70% of the men and women surveyed rate furniture, household appliances, electrical appliances and money as 'not good at all' or 'rather not good' (Statista 2021c, p. 17). In contrast, 85% of women (w) and 82% of men (m) consider flowers to be 'very good' or 'rather good', thus taking the top spot. Sweets/chocolates (81% w, 69% m), jewellery (75% w, 67% m) and perfume (74% w, 69% m) are also ranked highly. It seems remarkable that in second place after flowers with a restaurant visit is already an experience gift (87% w, 80% m) and that at least 61% of women also consider a voucher to be a suitable gift (but only 48% of men; Statista 2021c, p. 15). Also in Austria's "Top Ranking" of the most popular gifts on Valentine's Day 2021, 'vouchers' and 'experiences/excursions etc.' are among the five most popular gift categories from a list topped by 'flowers/plants' and 'chocolates/pralines/candy'; gifts on which Austrians spend an average of €72 that year – "more than ever" (Statista 2021a, p. 39).

With regard to the **motives and intentions** of romantic gift-giving, one might think that this is a case of acting out of altruism alone. However, this is not the case, especially when occasion-, trait- and gender-specific factors are included in the consideration. In this context, one can draw on the motive concept of Wolfinbarger (1990), who distinguishes between three groups of motives. Besides "altruism giving" as selfless giving without expectation of a return, these are "self-interested giving" as the intention to improve one's own situation and to avoid conflicts as well as obligation in the sense of adherence to social norms ("gift-giving as a norm"), be it the norm to give a counter-gift in the sense of the reciprocity rule, be it the norm to adhere to rituals, e.g. on certain occasions such as Christmas or a birthday (Goodwin et al. 1990).

With regard to the **specific occasion of Valentine's Day**, survey results are available for Germany that can be interpreted in terms of motives. In response to the question "For what reason do you celebrate Valentine's Day?", the following distribution of response categories was found in 2018: "To show my love": 80%, "Because it gives me pleasure to give gifts": 48%, "Because it has become a tradition": 27% and "Because it is expected of me": 9% (Statista 2021c, p. 3). Accordingly, the altruistic motive of expressing one's own love clearly dominates. The joy of giving a gift to a loved one also meets with a great deal of approval – by a wide margin – and can probably be assigned predominantly to this motive, possibly also partly to self-interest. However, it also becomes clear that external pressures such as general traditional or specific personal expectations prompt gift-giving and thus make it an obligation.

The extent to which this pressure is felt, joy is pushed back and the character of obligation comes to the fore, is apparently dependent on various influencing variables. In their study on gift giving in romantic relationships, Nguyen and Munch (2011) include situational factors and aspects of relationship quality as well as long-lasting and stable **personal predisposals**. In doing so, they refer to findings of attachment theory, which deals with the formation of close relationships based on early childhood experiences with the most important reference persons and the development of attachment relationships in the further course of life. They distinguish between secure, anxious and avoidant attachment types. While secure types are characterized by a positive self-concept and trust in the relationship, anxious and avoidant types constantly fear abandonment and neglect. Accordingly, attachment theory suggests that secure relationship types enjoy giving gifts more, which they see as an ideal means of showing their love, while anxious and avoidant types see gifts primarily as a necessary means of securing the relationship.

In addition, **gender-specific** differences also seem to play an important role. This is indicated by a US study by Rugimbana et al. (2003). The researchers examine the motives of young men for their Valentine's Day gifts, and here it emerges that the obligatory motive clearly dominates among the group surveyed. For the young men, gift giving on this occasion is, as one respondent puts it "something you just have to do" (Rugimbana et al. 2003 p. 69) because it is expected by their partner. It is also to this strongly felt sense of obligation that Otnes et al. (1994) attribute the fact that men have a less positive attitude towards the holiday than women. In addition to obligation, the motive of self-interest also seems to be stronger among men. For example, Saad and Gill's (2003, p. 769) study shows that men have more tactical-instrumental goals with their gifts than women, to show off their resources, to flaunt their generosity, or to use them as a means of seduction.

The research results presented on the motives cannot be reduced to a simple formula, but are nevertheless revealing. On the one hand, they show that all three groups of motives play a role and that they certainly cannot be precisely separated from one another, but are interwoven in a complex way. On the other hand, it becomes apparent that the type and cultural anchoring of the occasion as well as the personality traits and gender of the donor can also determine which constellation of motives predominates.

The **requirements for a gift** in romantic relationships are, of course, the same as those that characterize the perfect gift, including, most importantly, those that are required of any gift with a high emotional value: empathy, surprise, and sacrifice. However, these requirements are particularly high here. It is with gifts that are individually chosen for the partner with a high degree of **empathy** and that exactly match the state of the relationship that donors show the seriousness and depth of their feelings. It hardly needs to be stressed, therefore, that standard gifts of grey everyday usefulness – such as a mop bucket – are completely out of place in romantic relationships (Belk 1996, p. 64).

Like empathy, the **element of surprise** has an even greater role to play than usual in this context, as it is likely to trigger positive feelings of particular intensity in the recipient; and it is the recipient's emotional response that, in turn, also elicits strong emotions of pleasure and togetherness in the giver (Sherry et al. 1993; Gupta and Gentry 2019). Studies of gifts in dating relationships demonstrate the large impact of surprises. Respondents report that small surprise gifts with no formal occasion mean much more to them than more numerous and larger gifts on fixed occasions such as Christmas or birthdays (Belk and Coon 1993). And some large surprise gifts represent downright emotional high points in a romantic relationship. Gupta and Gentry (2019, p. 69) draw attention to our internal images of movie episodes in which a usually male lover opens a small square box to reveal an engagement ring, to which the usually female protagonist responds with highly emotional overwhelm. This scene apparently depicts the greatest and most meaningful surprise gift someone can receive from a loved one.

Even great **efforts and sacrifices** that givers take upon themselves to make the recipient happy with a gift are strong proofs of love, especially in romantic relationships.

This is shown particularly impressively in the famous Christmas story "The Gift of the Magi" by O'Henry. It is about two lovers who each make a great sacrifice in order to be able to give the other a gift, and it is these sacrifices that express their deep love.

> **O'Henry: The Gift of the Magi**
>
> This wonderful short story, first published in December 1905 in the Sunday supplement of what was then America's largest newspaper, the New York Sunday World Magazine, is about a young married couple, Jim and Della Dillingham, who are so poor that they can barely pay the rent on their small furnished apartment in New York. In no way do the two have enough money to give each other a real Christmas present.
>
> However, the Dillinghams own two things that are very precious to them. One is Jim's gold watch, inherited from his father and grandfather. The other is Della's shiny brown hair, which reaches below the back of her knees. In order to be able to give her Jim a nice present, Della gets herself to cut off her beautiful hair and sell it to a wigmaker. With the money she buys an expensive chain for his precious pocket watch.
>
> When Jim comes home, he stares at Della, stunned at first. For he has bought combs for her, which Della had long admired in a Broadway shop window. Beautiful expensive combs, pure tortoise shell with jewelled rims, which she had longed for but of course could never have dreamed of owning one day. To be able to purchase these expensive combs, Jim had sold his pocket watch.
>
> So both sacrifice for a gift with which they want to give the other great joy, which is very valuable and important to them, and at the same time actually make the other's gift useless. But because of the sacrifice, both are touched by the gift and are grateful as special evidence of their love. In the concluding paragraph, O. Henry relates this sacrificial gift-giving to the actions of the Wise Men from the East in the biblical Christmas story (O'Henry 1998).

The meaning and effect of gifts in romantic relationships also depend significantly on **the type of gift**. In gift research, various types are studied with regard to different aspects – such as 'joint', experiential and erotic gifts.

Huang and Yu (2000) focus on the fact that in romantic relationships different kinds of gifts are chosen depending on the primary addressee(s). Accordingly, they distinguish between "self-gifts", "other-gifts" and "joint-gifts". Self-gifts are primarily used to increase one's own attractiveness in the eyes of one's partner and thus one's self-esteem. Products such as perfume, cosmetics, clothing and other visible accessories are particularly suitable for this purpose. However, they are not taken into consideration here in accordance with the thematic restriction made. The "other gifts" are the usual gifts of symbolic communication with which partners assure each other of their love. The "joint gifts" are objects that both partners possess and which inform the outside world about the state of the relationship. As examples, the authors mention identical or matching watches or items of clothing worn by both partners (Huang and Yu 2000, p. 183).

The researchers explore the question of how the different types of gifts affect the duration or stability of a relationship. In their study, they conclude that "other gifts," which are private tokens of love, delay the dissolution of a relationship when the giver feels understood and validated by the recipient's response. However, if the giver perceives the response to the gift as disinterested or otherwise inappropriate, such gifts may actually hasten the timing of a relationship's dissolution. Deviating from this and unambiguously the effect of "joint gifts" turns out. The public and mutual demonstration of the relationship has a stabilizing effect, so that such joint gifts reduce the risk of the dissolution of a romantic relationship, at least in the student population studied.

Another type of gift in romantic relationships is attracting particular interest in research, namely **experience gifts**. These have a rather negligible material component and allow the partners to experience something special together. The above presented survey results on the most popular Valentine's Day gifts in Germany and Austria already indicate the importance of this type of gift, as 'restaurant visits' and 'excursions/experiences' are among the most frequently mentioned categories. Experience gifts include a wide range of options such as a visit to a concert or an exhibition, a day tour or a city break, a cruise or a mountain hike, a helicopter flight or a wellness weekend.

Even independent of romantic relationships, experience gifts are considered superior to material objects in that they lead to greater feelings of happiness and satisfaction. A whole range of reasons are offered to explain this superiority and have been empirically demonstrated (Van Boven and Gilovich 2003; Carter and Gilovich 2010; Caprariello and Reis 2013):

- Unlike material objects, experience gifts do not remain external, but often become a long-term part of one's own identity. A rich treasure of experiences makes for a richer life.
- Experience gifts do not become obsolete. New products don't stay new for long. A fashionable blouse is not fashionable for long. The current smartphone is very soon no longer up to date, then technically outdated, no longer compatible and in the end causes trouble so that it has to be replaced. A successful weekend in the mountains, on the other hand, remains a good memory for a long time.
- Experience gifts can actually gain over time as the experiences are embellished in memory. The efforts of a mountain hike are charged with pride and joy in retrospect and positively distorted. This is true even for originally nega-

tive events, such as the thundershower during the hike when one forgot to bring rain gear. Such incidents can become positive-value memories of challenges overcome; effects of this kind do not occur with material things.
- Experience gifts are more singular, less interchangeable and thus tend to be less comparable than a gift object. With a product, it is easy for the recipient to mentally compare qualitative and price alternatives. But no two hikes are completely alike.
- Experience gifts often have the most important characteristics for an optimal gift. They are often tailored to the exact wishes of the recipient with a high degree of empathy. They also usually contain an element of surprise, as one cannot anticipate all aspects of the experience, and the unexpected always occurs or can occur. In addition, surprise can still be integrated into the experience by not initially telling the recipient the details. In this case, the recipient is only asked to be ready and given information about necessary clothing and items to bring, some of which may be deceptive in nature to stage a greater surprise. Moreover, in many cases, experience gifts require a great deal of effort and time sacrifice, for example in the preparatory planning and organization. All this is rewarded by the recipient (Clarke 2007).
- Experience gifts have a social character. They are shared with others, family, friends and partners, which strengthens family, friendship and partnership bonds. And the experiences shared with others make one happier than material objects possessed alone and used only individually.
- The social character is also expressed in the fact that experiences are much more made the subject of conversations. One shares one's experience with others and thus also activates one's own and common experience again and again, which at the same time evokes and reinforces the positive emotions.

Obviously, all these reasons are strong arguments that experience gifts prove to be particularly suitable in romantic relationships, as empirical study results also confirm. Chan and Mogilner's (2017) research shows that the emotions associated with experience gifts are stronger than those associated with material gifts. And it is these strong emotions that have a particularly positive impact on perceived emotional relationship strength, i.e., increasing the extent to which partners feel close and connected to each other as well as satisfied with their relationship (Clarke 2007, 2013). This is also plausible, as emotions are not only generated when receiving the gift, but also still when experiencing the event itself, and in particular strength when the gift is experienced together with the partner. In addition, there is the aftereffect in the shared memory. Given this effect on the romantic relationship, it is only consistent for Van Boven and Gilovich to conclude their essay "To Do or to Have? That Is the Question" with the recommendation to donors to act according to the motto of an American nonprofit organization: "more fun, less stuff" (Van Boven and Gilovich 2003, p. 1201; Newdream 2021).

A very specific type of gift in romantic relationships is the focus of research by Nepomuceno et al. (2016): **erotic gifts**. They explore the extent to which the gifting of erotic products by men to women is hormone-driven, more specifically how prenatal testosterone as a masculine sex hormone affects men's romantic gifting in this regard. The finger length ratio, specifically the ratio of the length of the index finger (2D) compared to the length of the ring finger (4D), is considered an indicator of prenatal testosterone. A low value of the digit ratio 2D:4D corresponds to a high testosterone-estrogen ratio. Alternatively, the finger length ratio rel2, which relates the length of the four fingers to the index finger, is also used as an indicator and has been shown to be more valid in some studies. The authors use both criteria in their study.

There is a large body of research suggesting that men with a greater prenatal testosterone-estrogen ratio also exhibit more traits and characteristics considered typically masculine, such as aggressiveness or risk-taking. Applying this to aspects of consumer behaviour, Aspara and Van den Bergh (2014) show that men with a correspondingly low numerical ratio are also more likely to prefer products and colours with a masculine image. Based on these findings and the knowledge that men with high prenatal testosterone-estrogen ratios also have relatively strong sex drives, the researchers hypothesize that this hormonal nature also affects men's gift-giving behavior. In fact, their study proves that men with high prenatal testosterone-estrogen ratios feel a greater desire to give erotic gifts such as lingerie or erotic items to their partner. However, not all carry out this desire. Sex-related objects can lead to situations and feelings of embarrassment. Therefore, in the study, only men with a simultaneously high self-confidence in their ability to easily induce sexual contact also have the courage to put their intention to give erotic gifts into action.

Far less hormone-driven than in the time of first infatuation and young shared happiness in a beginning love are the romantic relationships in marriage and marriage-like **permanent relationships**.

Schiffman and Cohn (2009) examine the dynamics of gift-giving behaviour in married couples and show how this behaviour changes with the respective **phase in the life cycle** (e.g. the birth of children) and which constellations arise depending on whether there is agreement between the partners regarding the assessment of the financial or emotional value of gifts. Accordingly, the authors distinguish between two gifting rulebooks: the symbolic communication rules and the economic exchange rules. The symbolic rulebook corresponds to the understanding of gifts as symbolic communication and highly values all aspects of the emotional value of gifts such as empathy, surprise and effort. In contrast, the economic rulebook includes ideas about aspects of the financial value of gifts, strong attention to the resources used for this purpose, and rational as well as pragmatic considerations, including the use of money as a gift and precautionary consideration of exchange possibilities. If spouses use the same set of rules, this is not problematic. However, if they differ, then there is a valuation discrepancy. In this case, the authors identify three different strategies used by married couples:

1. Adjustment: Often it is the men who act according to the economic rules, but who (have to) learn to observe the symbolic rules desired by their wives and establish harmony by making an effort to behave in accordance with these rules.
2. Acceptance: Here, too, the partners follow different sets of rules. However, men follow all symbolic rules, while women do so only in their role as recipients. That is, when they receive gifts, it is the emotional value that counts for them, while they are more rational-pragmatic about their gifts for the husband, but this does not lead to conflicts because the latter accepts the approach.
3. Clash: Here no real adjustment or acceptance succeeds. Although women also try to teach men the symbolic rules here, they stubbornly resist the attempts to educate them. Since women see this as breaking the rules and expressing a lack of love, conflicts arise. If they cannot be resolved, women often accept this in the long run with a gender-specific justification: 'Just typical man'.

While addressing the situation of different valuation patterns in enduring relationships here, other researchers explore the question of how love changes in long-term relationships and how the change affects couples' romantic gift-giving. Minowa and Belk (2019) explore this question in in-depth interviews with older Japanese men and women, and they develop their concept of "**gorgic love**", which can be referred to as "**lasting love**" analogously.

This is not characterized by passion and physical attractiveness like erotic love, but by a more companionate affection, appreciation and care, based on shared experiences and values. The authors view this "gorgic love" model as a specific type of gift-giving that complements the typology of economic and social exchange and altruistic love presented in Chap. 2. Like the altruistic love ("agapic love"), lasting love ("gorgic love") differs from exchange theory concepts in that gift-giving is not selfishly focused on one's own benefit, but on the needs of the recipient. The gifts of lasting love, however, are different from those of altruistic love in that they are less expressively celebratory than empathically appreciative, less passionate than thoughtful, less idealistic than realistic, less altruistic than companionate. Moreover, they are often not only to be used individually by the recipient, but allow for sharing, which benefits the affectionate relationship (Minowa and Belk 2019, p. 45).

Their study shows that three dimensions of lasting romantic love can be distinguished: mature 'perfect gift' experience, distance of intimacy, and concern for well-being.

The **mature 'perfect gift' experience** in lasting love relationships can be characterized by appreciation, enriching everyday life, and simplifying.

Appreciation In long-term relationships, romantic gifts are a good opportunity to express appreciation towards the beloved partner. One feels the need to express gratitude for years of loyalty, support and help. Gifts express appreciation for each other's accomplishments in life together, accomplishments in work, home and child rearing, or simply for having been together through life's ups and downs for so long. In this situation, it is not so much about giving a big gift on specific occasions such as a wedding anniversary or birthday, but about loving gestures, expressed for example through flowers or an invitation to a nearby familiar restaurant.

Enrichment everyday life A 'perfect gift' in a relationship that is maturing is also when it helps to perceive life in a new way, to create opportunities for new sensory impressions and thus to enrich everyday life. Gifts of this kind are less about material goods and more about creating occasions for new shared experiences: an invitation to a new speciality restaurant, tickets for an evening at the theatre or a voucher for a short trip over the weekend. In all cases, the aim is to put the lasting relationship on an even broader footing and to change the style of the relationship in advancing years.

Simplifying The desire to make life less complex, to lighten the load and to reduce non-essential consumption can also influence gift giving. The giver refrains from using the gift to fill the usually already overflowing household with more things and looks for alternatives that make life easier and enable a less consumption-oriented lifestyle. Also, the desire to simplify supports the tendency to replace material things with gifts that enable shared experiences.

A second dimension of lasting love concerns **distance of intimicy**, which in turn can take place in three ways, through reflecting meaning in life, redefining relational closeness, and reminiscing.

Reflecting meaning in life In old age, one thinks more intensively about one's own life and the meaning of one's own existence, and occasions for gifts to one's partner are at the same time occasions for corresponding reflections, especially about the value of the personal relationship and closeness to the partner. Possibly, one's own role in the relationship is reflected upon, past failures are perceived more consciously, and the romantic relationship is seen in a changed light. Gifts can then be used to rehearse a new understanding of one's role, for example by encouraging the partner to pursue his or her hitherto postponed interests and hobbies, or by creating new opportunities for social contact, for example in the form of a group trip or joint activities in clubs and voluntary work.

Redefining relational closeness Reflecting on one's own life and relationship is linked to the fact that gift-givers reflect on and redefine closeness in the relationship at an older age. The closeness of the partners and their mutual dependence grow over time. Values that create identity are shared, perspectives converge. Such affectionate connections no longer need the proof of expensive gifts, so that from this motive, too, carefully chosen attentions and opportunities for shared experiences are sought, which further strengthen the emotional bond.

Reminiscing Romantic love in enduring relationships can also be expressed through gifts that recall love in the early stages of the relationship. This is usually done not so much by repeating earlier gifts, but by giving variations, usually in a toned-down or symbolic form. For example, the strong romantic feelings experienced on a trip to Paris years ago can be revived through a calendar of Paris photos, a souvenir or an invitation to a French restaurant.

The third dimension of lasting love is concern for well-being, as partners are aware of each other's physical limitations and therefore also use gifts to express their care and help their beloved cope with problems of aging. The study identifies four forms of this: Empathizing anti-aging, rejuvening, and preparing for aging.

Empathizing Donors are very aware of their partner's ailments and weaknesses and show their love by taking special care of their partner's physical and psychological impairments. Thus they choose as gifts health-promoting means and instruments as well as things that help to compensate for specific impairments, such as devices – like telephones – that are easier to use or have more legible lettering.

Anti-aging In a sense, gift givers are also trying to stop the aging process of their loved one with gifts. They give information and tools that allow the partner to proactively prevent possible frailty in old age and maintain control over their life for as long as possible. This can be done through mobility-enhancing tools or classes as well as books or games that present new mental challenges.

Re-juvening Anti-aging efforts increase when donors try to virtually reverse the aging of their partner or make it less visible. Cosmetic and pharmaceutical products in particular serve this purpose.

Preparing for aging Donors can use gifts to show the beloved ways in which they can manage their later life independently. Many who have lived in rigid role patterns for many years and rely entirely on their partner for various areas of life are disoriented and helpless when they are left to fend for themselves alone as survivors of a partnership. Therefore, it makes sense to acquire missing skills in time, but also to establish new social relationships and develop hobbies for leisure time. With appropriate gifts, donors can ensure that the loved ones will be able to maintain a high degree of independence and control over their life in the future, should they be the surviving partner.

Regardless of the degree to which these findings from a Japanese study are transferable to other cultures, they reveal essential, previously neglected insights. Romantic gift-giving is not only an issue in the passionate relationships of beginning love, but also in the long-term stable relationships of lasting love. Even though essential aspects of romantic gift-giving play a role in both phases, their content interpretation changes and weightings shift. Above all, gift motives and ideas about the perfect gift change, as surprise and effort tend to become less important over time, and empathy is more and more evident in gifts that express appreciation and caring, and allow for thoughtful lifestyle adjustments.

References

Aspara J, Van den Bergh B (2014) Naturally designed for masculinity vs. femininity? Prenatal testosterone predicts male consumers' choices of gender-imaged products. Int J Res Mark 31(1):117–121

Belk RW (1996) The perfect gift. In: Otnes C, Beltramini RF (eds) Gift giving: a research anthology. Bowling Green State University Popular Press, Bowling Green, pp 59–85

Belk RW, Coon GS (1993) Gift giving as agapic love: an alternative to the exchange paradigm based on dating experiences. J Consum Res 20(3):393–417

Caprariello PA, Reis HT (2013) To do, to have, or to share? Valuing experiences over material possessions depends on the involvement of others. J Pers Soc Psychol 104(2):199–215

Carter TJ, Gilovich T (2010) The relative relativity of material and experiential purchases. J Pers Soc Psychol 98(1):146–159

Chan C, Mogilner C (2017) Experiential gifts foster stronger social relationships than material gifts. J Consum Res 43(6):913–931

Clarke J (2007) The four 'S's' of experience gift giving behaviour. Int J Hosp Manag 26:98–116

Clarke JR (2013) Experiential aspects of tourism gift consumption. J Vacat Mark 19(1):75–87

Close A, Zinkhan G (2006) A holiday loved and loathed: a consumer perspective of Valentine's day. Adv Consum Res 33:356–365

Goodwin C et al (1990) Gift giving: consumer motivation and the gift purchase process. Adv Consum Res 17:690–698

Gupta A, Gentry JW (2019) If you love me, surprise me. In: Minowa Y, Belk RW (eds) Gifts, romance, and consumer culture. Routledge, New York, pp 65–79

Huang M-H, Yu S (2000) Gifts in a romantic relationship: a survival analysis. J Consum Psychol 9(3):179–188

Minowa Y, Belk RW (2019) Mature consumers. A storgic love paradigm. In: Minowa Y, Belk RW (eds) Gifts, romance, and consumer culture. Routledge, New York, pp 37–64

Nepomuceno M et al (2016) Testosterone & gift-giving: mating confidence moderates the association between digit ratios (2D: 4D and *rel2*) and erotic gift-giving. Pers Individ Differ 91(4):27–30

Newdream (2021) History. https://newdream.org/about-us. Accessed 20 Feb 2021

Nguyen HP, Munch JM (2011) Romantic gift giving as chore or pleasure: the effects of attachment orientations on gift giving perceptions. J Bus Res 64(2):113–118

O'Henry (1998) The gift of the magi. Alex Catalogue, Raleigh

Otnes C et al (1994) The pleasure and pain of being close: men's mixed feelings about participation in Valentine's day gift exchange. Adv Consum Res 21:159–164

Rugimbana R et al (2003) The role of social power relations in gift giving on Valentine's day. J Consum Behav 3(1):63–73

Saad G, Gill T (2003) An evolutionary psychology perspective to romantic gift giving among young adults. Psychol Mark 20(9):765–784

Schiffman LG, Cohn DY (2009) Are they playing by the same rules? A consumer gifting classification of marital dyads. J Bus Res 62(11):1054–1062

Sherry JF et al (1993) The dark side of the gift. J Bus Res 28(3):225–244

Statista (2021a) Ranking der Top 5 beliebtesten Geschenken am Valentinstag in Österreich 2021. https://de.statista.com/statistik/daten/studie/677199/umfrage/umfrage-in-oesterreich-zu-den-beliebtesten-geschenken-am-valentinstag/. Accessed 1 Feb 2021

Statista (2021b) Total expected Valentine's day spending in the United States from 2009 to 2021. https://www.statista.com/statistics/285028/us-valentine-s-day-sales/. Accessed 22 Feb 2021

Statista (2021c) Valentinstag in Deutschland und Österreich. https://www.statista.com/study_id59532_valentinstag.pdf. Accessed 23 Feb 2021

Van Boven L, Gilovich T (2003) To do or to have? That is the question. J Pers Soc Psychol 85(6):1193–1202

Wolfinbarger MF (1990) Motivations and symbolism in gift giving behavior. Adv Consum Res 17:699–705

8

Gifts to Different Recipients: Who Gets Anything at All and How Much?

For the big gift giving occasions like Christmas, there is usually more than one person to give a gift. There is a duty to give presents to all who attend the Christmas feast, and a decision has to be made as to which of them should get how much. With regard to those not present, this obligation is not so strict, and in some cases it even seems to be waived, so that the question arises whether a gift must or should be given at all. Again, there are **rules** to be followed in making these decisions. These are rules that are not laid down or taught anywhere, but which we have internalized during our socialization and which may only be violated within limits. These rules are closely related to the function of gifts as a medium of information. If gifts say important things about the nature and intensity of the relationship between the participants, then 'publicly' distributed gifts in particular must be considered in terms of their communication effect, since the information contained in gifts is sent to the entire closer family network (Lowrey et al.

2004). Accordingly, the gifts must be differentiated (scaled) in terms of value with regard to the respective status of the relationship.

Caplow (1984), in an empirical study in a small American town he calls Middletown (in reality it is Muncie in Indiana), has investigated which of these 'secret' scaling rules are observed at Christmas. Of course, such rules differ in various cultures, and they change when understandings of the holiday, of family, and of ways of living together change. Therefore, the rules lack actuality and cross-cultural validity. Nevertheless, they are presented here – with slight modifications and updates – because they still provide fundamental insights today and, moreover, can inspire everyone to reflect on which rule continues to be valid in one's own framework of action or is to be replaced by a different culture-, class- and family-specific variant. The focus is on the rules for various kinship relationships:

- **Married and marriage-like couples**: This relationship should be the most important for both partners. Accordingly, the most valuable gifts need to be exchanged here. In traditional couple relationships, where the man has a higher income, the man can give the partner a gift of higher value.
- **Children**: After the marital (and marriage-like) relationship, the parent-child relationship is the most significant. There must be no gradation between children, and this also applies to gifts. Children are therefore to be treated equally throughout life. This applies to the value of the gifts, but can also refer to the number of gifts and their symbolic meaning (Lowrey et al. 1996).

- **Daughters and sons-in-law**: Married partners of daughters and sons are as valuable to consider as their own children.
- **Parents**: Cohabiting fathers and mothers of adult children should be valued equally, possibly with slight advantages for the mothers. If father and mother are divorced, separated or otherwise married, the parents may be valued differently.
- **Siblings**: These should be valued equally in childhood, later differentiation is possible or common. Adult siblings who live nearby and are part of the family network should be valued equally along with their partners. Siblings who live further away and are only marginally linked to the network can be valued unequally.
- **Other relatives**: More distant relatives such as aunts, uncles or cousins can be assessed in much the same way as siblings (Caplow 1984).

Adherence to these scaling rules thus conveys messages such as "I value all my children equally," "I value my daughter-in-law as I value my son (as long as she is married to him)," or "I value my present brother more than the absent sister, but less than the parents and much less than my children" (Caplow 1984, p. 1320). In this way, the familial structure is made explicit and reinforced, and the gift rules are confirmed and reaffirmed.

One episode in Jonathan Franzen's voluminous successful novel "The Corrections" uses the example of the Lambert family to show that such Christmas gift rules are well known and provide orientation, but that there are also always reasons to deviate from these rules.

> **Jonathan Franzen: The Corrections**
>
> The novel centers on a planned and ultimately unsuccessful Christmas celebration of the Lambert family. Alfred Lambert is suffering severely and increasingly from Parkinson's disease and dementia. As a result, his wife Enid puts intense pressure on their adult children Gary, Chip and Denise to come home for one last Christmas. But there are problems. Only the youngest daughter Denise wants to fulfill her mother's wish without reservation. The eldest son Gary actually wants to come with his three children, Aaron, Cayleb and Jonah, but had promised his wife never to spend Christmas at the family home again. And Chip, an unsuccessful author, had refused to take part in the Christmas festivities for years.
>
> With the situation still unresolved, preparations begin. Alfred puts up the Christmas tree with a twenty percent tilt and tries to get the old fairy lights to work, while Enid writes umpteen Christmas cards and worries about allocating her gift budget. Her children, Densise and Chip, are each to receive a gift worth $100. For Chip, she has already purchased a $55 sale-priced brown-and-red wool bathrobe, so she only needs $45 worth of gifts for him. For her son Gary, however, she only plans for $60 worth of gifts. This deviation from the equality rule seems justified to her. After all, Gary is wealthy and, most importantly, he is married. Since the unloved daughter-in-law is to receive gifts (also for $60), the couple gets off easy. Regarding her grandchildren, Enid also overrides the equality rule: Aron and Caleb, whom she knows will not appear with their mother at Christmas, receive the same amount ($30). Jonah, who she hopes will accompany his father for the visit, is to be rewarded by a higher value gift this year (Franzen 2001, p. 473).

The fact that people make the conscious decision to **deviate from individual rules** is also shown by empirical research. In their longitudinal study of Christmas gift giving, for example, Lowrey et al. (2004) show that givers deviate from the principle of equal treatment for members of a recipient group, e.g. giving different gifts to siblings, because they want to express the respective degree of affection. They may also treat recipients from different groups in the same way. In this case, they give gifts to persons outside the close circle of the nuclear family (such as uncles or aunts) in the same way as they do to primary reference persons (e.g. parents), because they feel the same emotional closeness based on past experiences. The same certainly applies to gifts to friends, as friendships are often becoming more relevant, taking on a quasi-familial character (Dressel 2000) and also differing in terms of their emotional closeness.

The existence of rules of gift exchange, especially in family-public situations, already makes it clear that gift giving does not only take place in a dyadic relationship, i.e. between two participants at a time, but that **third parties** are involved in this process. In relation to gift giving decisions at Christmas, Lowrey et al. (2004) identify a variety of differentiated influences, with two types appearing particularly noteworthy: Gaining third party permission from gatekeepers and adhering to group norms. By **gaining permission** for a planned gift, donors demonstrate that they recognize the responsibilities of third parties to the recipient and that they intend to heed and respect their views. For example, asking parents if they agree if you plan to give their daughter a smartphone or their son a drum set seems appropriate. Similarly respectful is the **adherence to specific norms and rules** that apply to a group to which one belongs, regardless of whether these have come about without one's own involvement or whether they are an explicit agreement. Examples include agreements regarding a financial limit on gifts or an agreement to give gifts only to children this year.

The gift rulebook becomes even more complicated when **family situations change**. This is particularly the case when families break up due to divorce and new marriages or partnerships create changed family sets, such as patchwork families with children from different partners. As the family situation changes, so does the context for Christmas gift giving, as the number and types of people to be gifted varies, and many relationships are no longer the same. Even in 'unproblematic' new relationships formed through marriage, there is a need to communicate gifting norms or establish consensus if someone is making or planning changes. For example, one respondent in a British exploratory study of Christmas consumption rituals complained that she had given a small gift to her new sister-in-law after her marriage, but which was not well received. She was told in a less than friendly manner that in this family only the children were given presents at Christmas (McKechnie and Tynan 2006, p. 138). Out of ignorance, the new family member had not brought joy with her gift, but had broken a rule and was sanctioned accordingly.

Separations and divorces change the situation not only for the partners, but for all those in the former family **network** who want or need to remain in contact with one or more former family members. This includes adult children who have to cope with the new partners of their mother or father. Also affected are parents who, for example, want to maintain ties with their former daughter-in-law or son-in-law so as not to lose their relationship with their grandchildren. Gift-giving among **former partners** poses a particular problem. In this case, a very strong emotional relationship has ended, and former positive emotions lie buried under a lot of mutual hurt. Sometimes the parties involved have been separated for years and now live with other partners, yet ties remain or there are always occasions such as illness or the need for regulation. The lasting ties include above all the children, especially if the parents have joint custody or if one parent wants to maintain contact with the children growing up with the former partner.

In all these cases, gifts at Christmas can be associated with a variety of motives and fulfil different functions. They can be understood as a signal that the new situation and the new partner are accepted, or they demonstrate the attempt to integrate the new family member into the still existing system and to carry out a kind of assimilation. The focus may also be on showing children that despite the separation of the parents, nothing has changed in the basic relationship (Otnes et al. 1994).

Regardless of the motivation, gift rules must also be observed in new family arrangements so as not to open up old wounds and avoid new hurts:

- In many cases, the best solution for former **life partners** is to forego gifts. This is especially true when tensions still exist. But in general, this refrain can avoid any impression of wanting to endanger or influence a new relationship.
- Of course, if in the new constellation all get along well and even celebrate Christmas together, a gift is required. But this must not remind of the joint happy early days of love. So no photo book for memory, but also no voucher for the new couple to an event – a visit to a restaurant or a concert – that you used to visit together.
- **Children** living in their own household should be considered in the same way as those living in the partner family.
- Children of the new partner, own children and joint children are to be treated equally.
- A **former daughter-in-law or son-in-law** should be treated no worse than before, but no better than the son's or daughter's new partner.
- It seems permissible to give less to one's **mother's or father's new partner** than to one's mother or father, but the gift should signal by its value that one accepts the person and the situation as a child (Otnes et al. 1994).

The next fiction episode can be found in the book "Frank" by the American author Richard Ford, who writes about his multiple novel hero Frank Bascombe's experiences with old age, illness and death. The episode impressively shows the difficulties with gift giving in a long ended but never really ending relationship.

> **Richard Ford: Frank**
>
> Four days before Christmas, Frank Bascombe sets off in a snowstorm to an exclusive retirement home to deliver a gift to his ex-wife Ann Dykstra, who has Parkinson's disease. It is actually questionable whether "gift" is the right word, because to Frank it seems more like the delivery of an order. It is a special orthopedic pillow that neurologists in Switzerland recommend for homeopathic "treatment" of Parkinson's; a pillow she could just as easily have ordered online. When the door of Ann Dykstra's apartment opens, there is no personal greeting or hug. Ann simply steps back, as one would for a supermarket delivery service that knows the way to the kitchen. Frank places the plastic bag containing the pillow he was supposed to get on a chair. In the brief conversation that follows, there are isolated moments of closeness, but they are quickly drowned out by distance, abandonment, and loneliness, sometimes followed by sentences that sound like slaps in the face. At the end, Ann signals the end of "visiting time" by thanking him for bringing the pillow, still lying on the chair as he put it. "I was glad to," he replies, clearly aware that this sentence is a lie (Ford 2014, p. 174).

Giving gifts in family contexts is therefore particularly associated with ambivalent feelings. On the one hand, it is precisely here that one wants to express the specific closeness and give pleasure with gifts; on the other hand, one feels the pressure to fulfil the strict obligations of giving and to comply with the complex set of rules. In addition, the complexity of gift-giving increases with changes in the family situation and even in formally ended relationships the question of the right gift-giving is not conclusively answered.

References

Caplow T (1984) Rule enforcement without visible means: Christmas gift giving in Middletown. Am J Sociol 89(6): 1306–1323

Dressel G (2000) Gedanken zu einer Historischen Anthropologie des Gebens. In: Dressel G, Hopf G (eds) Von Geschenken und anderen Gaben. Annäherungen an eine historische Anthropologie des Gebens. Peter Lang, Frankfurt a. M., pp 13–29

Ford R (2014) Let me be frank with you. Harper Collins, New York

Franzen J (2001) The corrections. Farrar, Straus and Giroux, New York

Lowrey T et al (1996) Values influencing Christmas gift giving: an interpretive study. In: Otnes C, Beltramini RF (eds) Gift giving: a research anthology. Bowling Green State University Popular Press, Bowling Green, pp 37–56

Lowrey T et al (2004) Social influences on dyadic giving over time: a taxonomy from the giver's perspective. J Consum Res 30(4):547–558

McKechnie S, Tynan C (2006) Social meanings in Christmas consumption: an exploratory study of UK celebrants' consumption rituals. J Consum Behav 5(2):130–144

Otnes C et al (1994) In-laws and outlaws: the impact of divorce and remarriage upon Christmas gift exchange. Adv Consum Res 21:25–29

9

Difficult Givers and Recipients: Risk Reduction Strategies

Almost everyone knows it, and research confirms it: giving the right gift is not easy. However, it becomes particularly problematic in the case of difficult givers and difficult receivers.

Difficult givers are – in short – those who almost always give wrong gifts, do not notice this and therefore do not go through any learning processes. Selfishly, they think mainly of their advantage and put their interests and preferences in the foreground. They do not grasp the secret gift rules and therefore violate them again and again. They lack empathy, can't take the recipient's perspective, and don't realize what messages they are sending with their gifts. And – closely related to this – they lack "emotional understanding", i.e. the ability to perceive and understand the emotions in gift situations (Pillai and Sukumarakurup 2019). They are therefore unable to predict the recipient's emotional needs or correctly interpret the recipient's verbal and nonverbal signs of disappointment.

These difficult givers are responsible for much of the emotional wounds that can happen in gift exchange. It is they who, with their gift-giving behavior, create the risk that a relationship will be clouded or, in extreme cases, even ended. If it's a fairly loose relationship, such as between acquaintances who invite each other to large parties at long intervals at best, this isn't much of a problem. For one thing, the potential for disappointment is low, and for another, a relationship breakup is relatively easy to get over. With close partnership or family relationships, the problem is more serious. In one section of his Strindberg biography, the renowned Swedish writer Per Olov Enquist describes a scene in which August Strindberg gives his (third) wife Harriet a gift that shows a blatant lack of empathy and leads straight to disaster.

> **Per Olov Enquist: Strindberg. Ein Leben (Strindberg. A life)**
>
> Harriet sits on a suitcase and, crying, asks her husband why he won't keep his promise of a trip together. Strindberg answers his wife that traveling is not worth it. He had seen everything, such as the cities of Berlin, Paris or London. But there was nothing of value to see there. This does not convince Harriet, she wants to travel and see the world for herself. Then Stindberg takes out a small package and gives it to her as a gift, expecting to make her very happy. Hopefully, she unwraps the gift and holds a book labeled "Baedeker" in her hand. Strindberg explains that it is a travel guide that contains all the information about all kinds of places. With the Baedeker, she could save herself the hassle and inconvenience of traveling. Harriett is stunned. Outraged, she throws the guidebook across the room and screams that she will leave him now to go to Denmark, and runs out of the house.
>
> This episode is not yet the end of the marriage, but Harriet does not last long with the 29 years older and particularly difficult August Strindberg; the marriage is divorced after three conflict-ridden years. (Enquist 2012, pp. 238–240).

When cases are not quite so blatant and recipients do not want to sever their close ties with the difficult donor, they have few **strategic options to reduce risk**:

1. It is obvious that the recipient signals his or her own disappointment to the giver with clear words and signs and thus tries to influence the giver's behaviour in a positive way. However, if the personality traits described are strongly developed, the probability of success of this strategic variant is low. Such donors will not want to or be able to react even to strong signals. Strindberg, for example, did not change in response to Harriet's protest; he only turned to his 'Occult Diary' with anger and rage.
2. It promises more success to give the donor clear indications of what is desired in the preparation phase, preferably in writing and with detailed information on the best, i.e. easiest to implement and most cost-effective, procurement option. Since the giver is not to be presumed to be malicious, he is likely to take advantage of this opportunity to ease the burden of decision-making and save the recipient a disappointment.
3. If the recipient cares a lot about continuing the close relationship, e.g. with the partner or another family member, a psychological mechanism may also kick in to reduce dissonance due to repeatedly wrong gifts. This involves lowering expectations from the outset, or expecting a failed gift, so that only a low level of dissatisfaction can occur. A similar effect takes place when one subsequently values what one has received more highly because one now discovers certain advantages. In addition, it is obvious to attribute the gift-giving behaviour to the known personality of the giver, which is regarded as unchangeable. It is then necessary to accept this behaviour and to give it less weight in the light of other positive qualities.

While difficult givers can be characterized relatively uniformly, **difficult receivers** appear more differentiated. This is also shown by research results on Christmas gift-giving behaviour. For example, Otnes et al. (1992) conducted a study to investigate which of the gift recipients are considered difficult, why they appear difficult, and what gift selection strategies Christmas gift buyers choose to find gifts for difficult recipients. In their study, they identify different types of difficult recipients. However, their listing is logically unconvincing as they also list problems on the donor side and in the general conditions. Nevertheless, major types can be distinguished based on their research:

1. **The Wishless**: The people concerned emphasize that they neither need nor wish for anything. However, since they would be disappointed if they were not given anything at Christmas, it is particularly difficult to find a suitable gift.
2. **The Disinterested**: They are closely related to the wishless, but differ in the characteristic feature that they are not really interested in anything, have no hobbies and their favorite activity is idleness. For givers it is difficult to imagine what one can do to please such people.
3. **The Unknowns**: Although potential recipients are part of the circle of relatives and therefore should be considered, nothing or too little is known about them to develop ideas about possible wishes or appropriate gifts. This is especially true for people who are on the fringes of the circle, such as relatives by marriage.
4. **The Critically Picky**: Difficulties are also caused by recipients who are known for being very picky, having very narrow preferences and strongly held views (Cheng et al. 2014). Because they critically judge anything that does not exactly match their tastes, cultural expecta-

tions, or ideas of creativity, they fuel the fear of giving the wrong thing, making it difficult for donors to make a decision.

5. **The Whole-Other**: A similar situation occurs when the giver and receiver differ fundamentally in their interests and tastes. In this case, givers find it a problem to put themselves in the foreign world of imagination and to find exactly those objects which the recipient likes and which are also still missing in his or her special field of interest.
6. **The Restricted**: Recipients may be physically limited in their circumstances, such as having a medical condition affecting their vision, hearing, mobility, or food consumption, making many potential gifts ineligible.

In their study, Otnes et al. (1992) also examine how donors deal with this situation, i.e. what action strategies they choose. In doing so, they are primarily concerned with reducing their psychological risk, i.e. decreasing the psychological stress associated with gift selection, because one is constantly preoccupied with the gruelling gift problem for which there is actually no informational solution.

Basically, these strategies can be distinguished according to whether the donor's course of action is oriented primarily to the own person (giver-centered options) or to the person of the recipient (recipient-centered options) (Otnes et al. 1992).

Giver-centered gifting strategies include (1) delegation, i.e., delegating gift selection to another who is believed to be better able to choose the right gift. (2) orientation to one's own tastes or interests, and (3) community gifting, i.e., teaming up with one or more others, which can generate new ideas and also allows for other (such as more expensive) alternatives. (4) Another strategy is for donors to have a third party help them in their decision, for example by discussing and evaluating gift ideas with another person or by having someone accompany them when shopping for a gift (Lowrey et al. 2004).

Recipient-centric gift strategies represent (1) impulse buying, where there is a sudden 'epiphany' in the buying situation that a particular product might be the right thing to buy, and (2) habitual buying, choosing (almost) the same thing as last year or a slight variation of it that can be assumed to have had a satisfactory effect last year. In addition, (3) there is the opportunity to ask the 'unknowns', and especially the 'whole-other' and the 'critically picky' directly what they want, rather than trying to excite them (Cheng et al. 2014).

In another analysis of their study results, the authors (Otnes et al. 1993) explore the question of the extent to which the choice of strategy towards difficult recipients depends on the role that the donor takes towards the recipient (see Chap. 6). Of the roles identified, only the roles of 'pleaser', 'compensator' and 'acknowledger' are relevant with respect to this question. Acknowledgers, who only give gifts because they consider this act obligatory, are more likely to adopt giver-centred strategy variants. In contrast, pleasers, who make every effort to ensure that their gifts please the recipient, and compensators, who want to help the recipient overcome an experience of loss with a gift, primarily choose recipient-centered strategies.

Success is not guaranteed with any strategic action alternative. Giver-centered strategies already exclude by definition the orientation of gift considerations to the recipient. In recipient-centered strategies, only the direct request of wishes offers a solution with respect to some types of difficult recipients. However, all strategies primarily help the giver to reduce the psychological pressure of gift seeking. The basic social risk of making the wrong choice after all and thus damaging the relationship with the recipient remains. However, it is a risk for which the recipient – to varying degrees – is responsible.

References

Cheng A et al (2014) Choosing gifts for picky people: where is the fun in that? Adv Consum Res 42:22–23
Enquist PO (2012) Strindberg. Ein Leben. btb Verlag, München
Lowrey T et al (2004) Social influences on dyadic giving over time: a taxonomy from the giver's perspective. J Consum Res 30(4):547–558
Otnes C et al (1992) Ho, ho, woe: Christmas shopping for "difficult" people. Adv Consum Res 19:482–487
Otnes C et al (1993) Gift selection for easy and difficult recipients: a social roles interpretation. J Consum Res 20(2):229–244
Pillai RG, Sukumarakurup K (2019) Elucidating the emotional and relational aspects of gift giving. J Bus Res 101:194–202

10

Cash Gifts and Vouchers: When Are They Taboo and When Are They Welcome?

Money and vouchers are becoming increasingly popular in Germany. In a survey on Christmas 2020 regarding planned gifts, this category takes the top spot; 59% of respondents expressed the corresponding intention. Traditional Christmas gift classics such as books (55%), toys (49%), jewellery (29%) or cosmetics (28%) are far less popular (Statista 2021c, p. 55). The picture is similar in Austria and Switzerland. In response to the question "What do you prefer to give as a gift at Christmas 2020?", the answer category 'gift vouchers' received the most mentions in Austria (52%), followed at a great distance by 'children's articles and games' (24.8%) and 'books' (19.1%). In fourth place comes 'cash' (17%; Statista 2021b, p. 8). In a slightly older survey for Switzerland (2018), the category 'gift voucher/money' takes fourth place in the gift ranking with 52% (Statista 2021a, p. 13).

These data are surprising in that **gifts of money** have an **ambivalent character**. They can have advantages in economic-financial terms for both giver and recipient, but have disadvantages in terms of the symbolic dimension, the emotional value of the gift.

Economists see only **advantages** in gifts of money. A giver who has sufficient disposable financial resources does not have to worry about a suitable gift. He is – as the French sociologist Pierre Bourdieu (1998, p. 99) writes – relieved of the work of symbolic construction: "For example, when, instead of giving a 'personal' present, that is, a present adjusted to the presumed taste of the reciever, one gives, through laziness or convenience, a check, one economizes the work of looking, which assumes the attention and care necessary for the present to be appeared to the person, to his or her tastes". Recipients who are primarily economically minded receive funds that they are free to use according to their preferences, and they can therefore ensure that they do not receive unwanted gifts. In the case of gifts in kind, on occasions such as Christmas or weddings, when many people give gifts at the same time, it happens that identical gifts are given, so the recipients receive duplicate gifts unnecessarily (Cheal 1996). This is avoided with a monetary gift. There is also the fact that givers often spend more on a gift than the recipient would have spent on that product itself. For economists, this makes the preference for gifts in kind irrational and inefficient. The most prominent proponent of this position is the American economist Joel Waldfogel (1993, 1998). If, he argues, an individual gives away a sweater worth $50, but it is worth at most $25 to the recipient, then there is a $25 loss in value that could have been avoided with a cash gift. Preferring gifts in kind and avoiding cash gifts thus appears to be a total economic welfare loss of considerable magnitude. According to Waldfogel's calculation, this loss is said to amount to between 10% and one-third of Christmas gift spending alone, and therefore to reach double-digit billions. Accordingly, in his publications he strongly advises against the usual value-destroying gift-giving: "Why you shouldn't buy any presents for the Holidays" (Waldfogel 2009).

What economists overlook in this argument, however, are the **detrimental symbolic meanings** of monetary gifts (Burgoyne and Routh 1991). Money fully exposes the material character and financial value of a gift. Typically, however, the economic-commercial connotations associated with money are unwanted in gifts. To avoid such unwelcome connotations, visible price information on the product, such as a book, is usually pasted over. Also, money does not give an opportunity to express specific feelings about the recipient and the emotional appreciation of the relationship (Prendergast and Stole 2001). Money has none of the qualities associated with a successful gift, such as the effort of consideration, selection, or wrapping. And this lack of personal effort devalues a gift of money from the recipient's perspective, or may even make it morally dubious (Cheal 1987, 1988). Even more significant often seems to be the fact that money takes away the memory effect of the gift. The givers lose any identification with the gift given; and if they do not receive any feedback, they do not know, even in retrospect, what they actually gave (McGrath and Englis 1996). The recipients' identification with the gift is also usually low, since they hardly mentally associate what they later buy with the giver and it does not remind them of him or her (Cheal 1987).

These disadvantages of monetary gifts are matched by the **advantages of gifts in kind**: only with a gift in kind can givers illustrate the thought they have put into fulfilling the recipient's wishes. Only with a gift in kind can they communicate their personal commitment, their sacrifices, and also information about themselves and the state of the relationship. Only with a gift in kind can they show that they know and adhere to social conventions, for example, by bringing flowers or a bottle of wine as a gift as a guest rather than a bank note. For these advantages, many people apparently accept the economic disadvantages of gifts in kind. Economists interpret the associated inefficiencies as a price that people pay in order to endow the gift with the desired symbolic value and to be able to demonstrate affection to the recipient (Camerer 1988; Cameron 1989).

In view of the increasing popularity of monetary gifts, the question arises as to whether this expresses a fundamental social change in the evaluation of the listed advantages and disadvantages. It is natural to speculate whether economic thinking is gaining in importance. It is quite conceivable that donors find the prospect of efficiency gains and the savings in time and thought increasingly more attractive than the recipient's expected pleasure in an emotionally valuable gift. Similarly, it may be that recipients are increasingly interested in money instead of things chosen with care for them. But such conjectures are speculative and cannot be based on empirical evidence. In addition, it is observable that even with a probably growing general acceptance of monetary gifts, differentiations must be made. Obviously, depending on the occasion, the type of relationship and the relative financial status of those involved, they are more or less welcome or even taboo.

Empirical studies show that gifts of money only appear to be appropriate or even desired on comparatively few **occasions**. One such occasion is weddings (McGrath and Englis 1996), where it may be regionally customary or even explicitly requested by the inviting couple to give money. An important reason for this is that it is intended to defray the costs of the wedding celebration, so that the guests at least pay for the banquet in this way. It is also conceivable that the bride and groom already have household equipment in their previous single or joint couple life. Then they can achieve with the money wish that nothing useless, unwanted or duplicated is given to them and that they have an amount at their disposal which they can use for another great wish, for example a special honeymoon (Cheal 1988).

On other occasions – such as birthdays or Christmas – money is by no means always appropriate as a gift. In a Christmas gift exchange, the gifts are placed in a specific cultural context and, through quasi-ritual measures such as elaborate packaging and a consciously meaningful handover, are set apart from the profane world of products and become a quasi 'sacred' object in the sense of something special and worthy of veneration (Belk et al. 1989). Banknotes are not very suitable for this.

However, if monetary gifts are to be used, then again there are some valid, unquestioned and usually unconscious rules to consider (Caplow 1982; Burgoyne and Routh 1991), which relate to the nature of the relationship and the relative status of those involved.

In the **relationship** between (married) **partners**, a gift of money at Christmas or on a birthday is an absolute taboo. It is completely inappropriate when the husband opens his wallet under the Christmas tree and hands over a note. The dreariness can only be increased if both partners exchange envelopes with banknotes on this occasion. With such a mutual gift of money, the reciprocity rule also immediately kicks in, i.e. it becomes embarrassingly obvious who gave the smaller gift of money. In most cases, those who receive more money from their partner than they gave will find this situation more humiliating than a financial gain in exchange. Merry Christmas is not to be expected here. That is why this type of behavior hardly ever occurs.

Different norms apply to relationships between **other family members**, especially if they are unequally endowed in financial terms. Empirical studies of monetary gifts in real life show that they come quite predominantly from older relatives such as parents or grandparents, while the latter do not usually receive monetary gifts. Apparently, one rule is that whoever gives money should be **superior in terms of age and/or status** (Caplow 1982; Burgoyne and Routh 1991). Accordingly, it is not only norm-compatible but usually highly desirable when, for example, **grandparents** express their generosity to their student grandchildren through a gift of money. This is especially true when the grandchild wants to fulfill a big, expensive dream, such as a trip or study abroad, a dream that can only be fulfilled if relatives provide financial support. It is not necessary that the grandparents find the gift of money easy. On the contrary, especially when the recipient knows that the giver is making a financial sacrifice, the monetary gift acquires an additional high symbolic value.

By contrast, corresponding behaviour in the opposite respect is usually regarded as inappropriate and irritating, for example when student children give their parents a gift of money, especially if the latter primarily finance the children's living expenses (Burgoyne and Routh 1991). Even when adult children are in a better financial situation than their parents and want to support them, it is not very appropriate to provide this support in the form of monetary gifts on special occasions. Giving a bank note instead of a bouquet of flowers on Mother's Day is sure to cause irritation rather than joy.

The rule of age and/or status superiority of the giver implies, in the case of age-matched partners, the symbolic information that the recipient is in a status and financially inferior position. To avoid this message, money is almost never used as a gift among **friends** (Burgoyne and Routh 1991). The problem of (overly) generous gifts among **siblings** has already been pointed out. This problem is particularly great in the case of gifts of money. Those who demonstrate their status superiority over siblings in euros and dollars by giving a large financial amount are more likely to trigger feelings of humiliation rather than gratitude.

People who are on the **fringes of the family network**, such as distant **uncles and aunts**, are usually hardly aware of the interests and wishes of their nieces and nephews. Therefore, even in view of their undoubted superiority in terms of age and status, it is obvious and appropriate for them to make gifts of money to children, if necessary after consultation with the parents. This applies primarily to older children, who are usually very happy about this, because it prevents them from getting something completely unwanted or banal from their point of view, and now have all the freedom they need to obtain something they have longed for since long time, or to fulfil newly arisen wishes. For them, sums of money are 'gifts of freedom' (Schmid 2017, p. 22). And it is this freedom of use that, from the perspective of purely economically arguing authors, makes these gifts from people less close to the recipient seem much more efficient than non-money gifts from close family members (Waldfogel 2009). For monetary gifts avoid value destruction and in many cases lead to high satisfaction. This is especially true for individuals who have a strong orientation toward efficiency and money, as is the case with Jill and Betty Trevor in a Christmas story by De Horne Vaizey.

> ### G. De Horne Vaizey: Betty Trevor
>
> This story is about the behavior of Betty Trevor and her siblings Jill, Jack, and Pam during the Christmas season. Jill manages to be extremely efficient and economical during Advent, taking care of fifteen presents in one afternoon by refilling her mother's old boxes of chocolates and perfume bottles with cheap substitutes. She then writes precautionary thank-you notes to all the relatives from whom she expects gifts, thanking them effusively but leaving blanks so that she can later fill in the gift she actually received.
>
> She is asked to name a wish of her own by a friend of the house, old General Digby, who surprises her in the process

> and whom she had not even thought of as a possible donor. But she can't decide, because she actually wants everything she can get.
> On Christmas Day after returning from church, the children's eyes fall on a stack of Christmas cards. By feeling the envelopes, they quickly suspect that they might contain money. In fact, General Digby has given them all a gift of money. So Jill receives a new ten-shilling piece and she is totally thrilled: "It's what I like better than anything else, to be rich in the Christmas holidays!" (De Horne Vaizey 2007).

In De Horne Vaizey's story, money gifts in the form of valuable coins make a big impression; Betty gets a "brand new gold thaler," Pam a "splendid silver thaler." Modern gifts of money usually turn out far less splendid and shiny. The most mundane is to simply transfer the amount to the bank account, but more usual is to hand it over in an envelope. When this is opened, whether immediately or often later, the note it contains should also be in good condition – preferably new. People appreciate clean and new banknotes, while those in (very) used condition appear contaminated (Di Muro and Noseworthy 2013), which has a negative impact on the valuation of the gift and even on the perception of the monetary value.

An only slightly disguised variant of the monetary gift are **vouchers** which the recipient can redeem for a gift, whereby the maximum amount of money is precisely defined. Such vouchers have some of the same **disadvantages** as pure cash gifts. So also here the precise monetary value becomes obvious and makes an economic evaluation of the financial employment and possibly the relationship strength possible. In this context, as with direct cash gifts, the nominal amount of the voucher is often perceived as less valuable by the recipient because the "cash stigma" acts psychologically like a tax, so that a $100 voucher, for example, only seems like an $80 gift to the recipient (Waldfogel 2009, p. 61).

Moreover, the flexibility of spending money is limited by the specification of the company at which the redemption must take place. In this respect, this variant appears at first glance to be even more problematic than a pure cash gift. Nevertheless, they receive comparatively more acceptance (Webley and Wilson 1989; Webley et al. 1983).

The reason for this is that gift vouchers can be specifically targeted to the needs and desires of the recipient (Burgoyne and Routh 1991). A purposefully chosen voucher for a meal at the recipient's favourite restaurant or for a visit to a museum or concert preferred by the recipient signals the giver's thoughtful engagement with the person of the recipient and empathy. In this case, the voucher also has the added **benefit** for the giver of activating good memories of him or her when redeemed. However, the voucher must also be redeemed, but in many cases this is not or only partially the case. Unredeemed vouchers generate millions in profits for the retail sector every year, which, although not a destruction of value, means that the gift is not given to the recipient – as planned – but to the retail groups (Waldfogel 2009).

Without the disadvantages of the monetary character and without target conflict problems are vouchers with which givers themselves offer their time or service, such as 3 × babysitting, wood chopping or a computer course. If vouchers of this type are actually targeted to the needs of the recipient and also make sense in terms of the skills, promised commitment and, if applicable, financial restrictions of the giver, they will trigger joy. In addition, there is the anticipation of the helpful contacts and joint activities to be expected in the future.

With regard to redemption, there are different obligations for monetary vouchers and non-monetary vouchers. In the case of monetary vouchers, it is the recipient's responsibility to ensure that the voucher is redeemed. It is also recommended that the giver is informed about the redemption and the positive emotions it triggers. In the case of non-monetary time and service vouchers, the situation is different. Here, it is often embarrassing for the recipient to claim the promises made. Therefore, it is the duty of the givers to approach the recipient and make appointments. If they fail to do so and the gift voucher 'expires' by the next Christmas, then the gift that was initially so gladly received appears to be an obviously not serious, easily achievable embarrassment solution. The recipient feels deceived and hopes not to receive such a voucher again next Christmas.

References

Belk RW et al (1989) The sacred and the profane in consumer behavior: theodicy on the odyssey. J Consum Res 16(1):1–38

Bourdieu P (1998) The economy of symbolic goods. In: Bourdieu P Practical reason. Polity Press, Cambridge, pp 92–123

Burgoyne CB, Routh DA (1991) Constraints on the use of money as a gift at Christmas: the role of status and intimacy. J Econ Psychol 12(1):47–69

Camerer C (1988) Gifts as economic signals and social symbols. Am J Sociol 94(Supplement: Organizations and institutions: Sociological and economic approaches to the analysis of social structure):180–214

Cameron S (1989) The unacceptability of money as a gift and its status as a medium of exchange. J Econ Psychol 10(2):253–255

Caplow T (1982) Christmas gifts and kin networks. Am Sociol Rev 47(3):383–392

Cheal D (1987) Showing them you love them: gift giving and the dialectic of intimacy. Sociol Rev 35(1):150–169

Cheal D (1988) The gift economy. Routledge, London

Cheal D (1996) Gifts in contemporary North America. In: Otnes C, Beltramini RF (eds) Gift giving: a research anthology. Bowling Green State University Popular Press, Bowling Green, pp 85–97

De Horne Vaizey (2007) Betty Trevor. https://www.gutenberg.org/files/21117/21117-h/21117-h.htm. Accessed 8 Feb 2022

Di Muro F, Noseworthy TJ (2013) Money isn't everything, but helps if it doesn't look used: how the physical appearance of money influences spending. J Consum Res 39(6):1330–1342

McGrath MA, Englis B (1996) Intergenerational gift giving in subcultural wedding celebrations: the ritual audience as cash cow. In: Otnes C, Beltramini RF (eds) Gift giving: a research anthology. Bowling Green State University Popular Press, Bowling Green, pp 123–141

Prendergast C, Stole L (2001) The non-monetary nature of gifts. Eur Econ Rev 45(10):1793–1810

Schmid W (2017) Vom Schenken und Beschenktwerden, 2nd edn. Insel Verlag, Berlin

Statista (2021a) Weihnachten in der Schweiz. https://www.statista.com/study_id31438_weihnachten-in-der-schweiz-statista-dossier.pdf. Accessed 25 Feb 2021

Statista (2021b) Weihnachten in Österreich. https://www.statista.com/study_id31498_weihnachten-in-österreich-statista-dossier.pdf. Accessed 25 Feb 2021

Statista (2021c) Weihnachtsgeschäft in Deutschland. https://www.statista.com/study_id7662_weihnachten_statista-dossier.pdf. Accessed 8 Feb 2021

Waldfogel J (1993) The deadweight loss of Christmas. Am Econ Rev 83(5):1328–1336

Waldfogel J (1998) The deadweight loss of Christmas: reply. Am Econ Rev 88(5):1358–1359

Waldfogel J (2009) Scroogenomics: why you shouldn't buy presents for the holidays. Princeton University Press, Princeton

Webley P, Wilson R (1989) Social relationships and the unacceptability of money as a gift. J Soc Psychol 129(1):85–91

Webley P et al (1983) The unacceptability of money as a gift. J Econ Psychol 4(3):223–238

11

Handling Over and Receiving the Gift: The Moment of Truth

When the gift is given and received, it is decided whether the goal of triggering joy is achieved or not. Therefore, this exchange situation is the 'moment of truth' in the gift-giving process.

Interestingly, this usually brief moment already influences the behavior of the participants before it occurs. As a mental anticipation, it already plays a role in the **preparation phase**. This is because the anticipation of the recipient's joy at receiving the gift influences the donors' commitment, their search strategies and also their gift decision. Thus, it is believed that givers care most about the recipient's immediate emotional reaction and less about the recipient's subsequent satisfaction, especially for gifts that are given directly. Yang and Urminsky (2018) refer to this assumption as "smile-seeing hypothesis". According to this hypothesis, this striving for the recipient's smile leads givers to choose gifts that they assume will spontaneously trigger more joy when unwrapping. At the same time, they neglect the fact that recipients might be more satisfied overall with another gift that has advantages when used later. This behavior appears rational from their perspective. For they cannot observe any later satisfaction on the part of the recipient; in most cases, they will hear little or nothing about it at all. Smiles and exclamations of enthusiasm on the part of the recipient when the object directly handed over becomes visible, on the other hand, are immediately experienced by them as evidence of the successful gift. It therefore also seems plausible that givers sometimes deliberately deviate from the recipient's preferences (Galak et al. 2016). Thus, the "smile-seeing hypothesis" is used as another explanation for donors preferring gifts in kind to cash, even when recipients would actually prefer money. According to this hypothesis, donors make this decision as long as they assume that cash gifts elicit weaker affective responses (Gino and Flynn 2011; Yang and Urminsky 2018).

Part of the mental and practical preparation for the 'moment of truth' is also the **wrapping**. According to the "wrapping rule" (Caplow 1984, p. 1310), gifts, especially on formal occasions such as Christmas or birthdays, must be wrapped before they can be handed over. Various reasons play a role in this. Cheal (1987) points out that most gifts today are mass-produced industrial products that offer little opportunity to charge them with individual messages. In order to identify these interchangeable products as gifts, they have to be personalized and marked in certain ways. The packaging serves this purpose. For a moment, attention is drawn not to the content but to the fact that it is a gift. Most importantly, the function of packaging is to heighten anticipation and excitement, and to allow for surprise. Even items that are difficult to wrap – such as a bicycle – are then symbolically wrapped, for example by bows or a blanket, and moreover hidden until they are handed over (Caplow 1984, p. 1309). The same applies to experience gifts, such as travel and leisure activities, which, as intangible things, cannot be packaged. The corresponding airline tickets, hotel vouchers or concert tickets are at least 'hidden' in an envelope, which is sometimes placed in yet another package in order to steer the recipient's imagination in the wrong direction and towards a possible material object (Clarke 2007, 2013).

When the **moment of gift exchange** arrives, it is also the packaging that gives a first impression of the gift. With children, this is of little importance. For them, the packaging is usually nothing more than an expectation-raising obstacle that is overcome as quickly as possible in a destructive manner. With adults, however, the packaging is a sign that is evaluated in many details. For example, the quality of the paper, the appropriateness of the motif for the occasion in question, and the additional use of ribbons, bows, stickers or tags all play a role. Likewise, the care with which the gift is wrapped and whether the givers have taken action themselves or used the professional wrapping service of a retailer is usually perceived.

In view of this symbolic character and the communication effect of the packaging, many givers go to great lengths and also incur costs in order to be able to present a properly wrapped gift. They assume that recipients expect just that, and some are also dissatisfied with the result because the appearance of the gift they have wrapped does not turn out as well as they imagined and consider necessary for the recipient. In these considerations and activities, donors assume that there is a "**spillover effect**" in the sense that beautiful packaging radiates positively on the evaluation of the gift and less attractive packaging has a negative effect on the evaluation of the gift.

The questions as to whether this effect actually exists and, if so, how strong it is, have so far received only few and, moreover, inconclusive answers in research. Howard (1992) states in several experiments that the packaging of a gift clearly positively influences the attitude of the recipient to the object received. He explains this effect theoretically by saying that wrapped gifts evoke memories of past moments of happiness and joyous occasions with gifts that were usually wrapped, such as childhood birthdays. And these reactivated feelings put the recipient in a happy mood, which biases the evaluation of the gift in a positive direction. His empirical studies also show that happy mood and influence on the perception of the gift are stronger when the gift is wrapped in traditional wrapping paper and given on a ritual occasion, such as a birthday.

But whether this effect occurs in every case is not disputed. Obviously, the effect of packaging on the recipient seems to be more complex than initially assumed. As Rixom et al. (2019) show in their studies, packaging arouses expectations with regard to the gift, can therefore increase or decrease expectations and in this respect influence the recipient's perception and satisfaction. Recipients have higher expectations of a gift at the sight of elaborate, beautiful and careful packaging than at sloppily packaged ones. These findings thus also confirm a kind of spillover effect, but only in relation to the recipient's expectations. However, the researchers focus their research on situations where the expectations raised are not confirmed. Now it turns out that unconfirmed expectations have an opposite effect on the evaluation of the gift ("**contrast effect**"). If the expectation raised by the packaging is not fulfilled after unwrapping, this has a negative effect on the evaluation of the gift and the satisfaction of the recipient. If, on the other hand, shoddy packaging reduces the expectation of the gift and the gift then turns out to be very nice, then this disconfirmation of expectation has a satisfaction-increasing effect.

However, one can only derive from these results the recommendation to avoid excessive luxury packaging that does not correspond to the gift. In contrast, the conclusion makes little sense or is more than risky to lower expectations through careless packaging in order to achieve a higher rating and satisfaction by exceeding expectations when unwrapping. On the one hand, it is not essential that the desired contrast effect occurs at all; on the other hand, the type of packaging not only influences expectations regarding the gift, but also conveys information about the givers, their taste, and the effort and care they have taken. The choice and use of paper specially suited to the occasion, the decorations and inscriptions applied, the use of ribbons and bows, all say something about the effort made by the givers, their sacrifice of financial resources and time, and thus also give indications of the relationship status.

In this respect, the much used practice of donors to pay attention to packaging seems quite justified. This also applies in view of current considerations of expressing one's own sustainability awareness from an ecological point of view by declaring the packaging rule to be obsolete and choosing the 'unpackaged solution'. Because often the advantages of a good ecological conscience and a corresponding self-portrayal of the giver achieved in this way are offset by the disadvantage of lower or missing positive emotions on the part of the recipient.

The actual **delivery** of the wrapped gift places clear demands on both giver and recipient and is associated with significant risks (Belk and Coon 1993; Otnes et al. 1993; Austin and Huang 2012). The giver has to accompany the presentation with a personal address to the recipient; the recipient has to receive the gift with joy, unwrap it with great attention, and then show positive surprise and gratitude. So not only the giver has to fulfil certain wrapping duties, but the – adult – recipient has to observe corresponding unwrapping duties. 'He may show emotions of uncertainty, nervousness and curiosity, he may be clumsily when unpacking, but at the dramatic climax, he must express his surprise and joy' (Berking 1996, p. 25). To avoid getting it wrong here, one must practice. Maruan Paschen shows this in his work "Weihnachten: Ein Roman" (Christmas: A Novel).

> **Maruan Paschen: Weihnachten: Ein Roman (Christmas: A novel)**
>
> In this Christmas novel, the protagonist describes how he was literally schooled by his mother in terms of proper unwrapping. Until now, he had always simply torn down the wrapping paper. But his mother then explained to him that it was a gesture of appreciation to unwrap gifts with care. So she lets him practice unwrapping. To do this, she very carefully wraps a lunch box with newspaper, first shows him how to receive the wrapped gift with great interest and how to make initial guesses about the contents. Then it is a matter of carefully removing the adhesive tapes without tearing the wrapping paper. Finally, she teaches him how to react correctly when he recognizes the gift, namely by convincingly signaling his surprise and delight with "ohs" and "ahs" (Paschen 2018).

Because unwrapping and recognizing the gift is such a special moment, especially at Christmas, recipients like to be photographed in this situation, in the moment of real or feigned excitement (Caplow 1984).

However, if the recipient's expectations are not met and there can be no question of enthusiasm, emotional work in the sense of managing one's own emotions is required (Hochschild 2012; Taute and Sierra 2015), because rules of politeness and social norms dictate that no signs of disappointment should be shown. Cultural standards require that the recipient not only silently endures the ordeal of negative emotions, but displays the required opposite feelings of joy and gratitude (Sherry et al. 1992).

However, compliance with this requirement is by no means always successful, as recipients communicate their negative feelings in various ways without always being aware of them. **Three communication channels** in particular play an important role here (Roster 2006):

- **Visible facial expressions and gestures:** raised eyebrows, a freezing smile or a facial expression that does not match the verbally expressed joy make the actual assessment clear.
- **Audible reactions:** when recipients make immediate references to the unsuitability of the gift or ask questions that indicate a lack of understanding ("What do you do with it?") they show that their expectations have not been met. The same is true if the gift received is commented on with a tone in the voice that is at odds with the enthusiasm presented. The absence of comments can also be telling, for example if the gift is received without thanks or positive comments.
- **Dealing with the gift:** disregard for a gift becomes clear immediately after it has been given, when it is carelessly placed. In the medium term, it manifests itself in the refusal to use or display what has been received. This is the case, for example, when items of clothing are never worn or vases are hidden in the cellar, disposed of or given away (Roster and Amann 2003; Roster 2006).

One can assume that donors decode such messages of disappointment. This is because they observe the recipient's reaction with great attention and look for clues as to whether he or she was really happy or just trying to hide the disappointment. When the absence of pleasure cannot be ignored, it immediately triggers disappointment or other negative emotions such as guilt and shame in the giver (Sherry et al. 1992). This implies the important insight that not only the behaviour of the giver, but also to a large extent the emotional reaction of the receiver to the gift determine whether gift giving intensifies or weakens the relationship.

Of course, it is also conceivable that disappointed recipients may forgo deceptive strategies and honestly express their lack of satisfaction. In an exploratory study by Roster and Amann (2003), respondents in their role as recipients indicate that they value honesty and that they view the ability to speak openly about failed gifts as an expression of a trusting relationship. But in the role as donors they cite a number of factors that more or less prevent them from acting honestly – as actually preferred. Still comparatively easy, honest feedback seems to be in familiar, close, but not romantic relationships. But even there, honesty is apparently difficult when the giver has put considerable investment into the selection, presentation, and symbolic meaning of the gift. Equally inhibiting to honest negative feedback is the fear that, given the gift givers' individual characteristics, one should expect them to react offended and hurt. In this respect, at the moment of truth, a norm-violating, openly articulated negativ truth is rarely to be expected.

The moment of gift receipt is significant not only because of the momentary emotional impact, but also because these emotions have **after-effects**. Ruth et al. (1999, 2004) examine these after-effects in terms of the relationship between the participants. Using in-depth interviews and surveys using the critical incident method, they ask subjects to describe particular gift-giving experiences and provide information for the short- and long-term consequences of the gift for the relationship. Based on the responses, they identify six relationship effects in the use phase where a relationship adjustment occurs.

- **Strengthening**: the relationship takes a positive turn through the gift, i.e. gains in intensity and depth, which often succeeds in particular through gifts with high symbolic meaning.
- **Affirmation**: the gifts reinforce a good relationship without elevating it to a higher level by reproducing existing bonds of friendship and family.
- **Negligible effect**: the gift does not change the relationship, or hardly changes it, either positively or negatively.
- **Negative confirmation**: here the gifts prove to be further evidence of an existing bad relationship. As in the past, the recipient learns that there is a lack of feelings of connection and shared values and interests, but this does not lead to a further deterioration of the relationship.
- **Weakening**: the gifts arouse strong negative feelings such as anger, discomfort or embarrassment. This is particularly the case if the gift is perceived as insulting or disrespectful, is interpreted as a kind of bribe, or is implicitly linked to the expectation of an unpleasant specific quid pro quo. Here the perceived relationship quality shifts in a negative direction.
- **Severing**: in very rare cases, gifts also lead to the immediate dissolution of relationships. However, this only occurs in extreme situations, for example when gifts are perceived as part of a stalking strategy or as a threat.

Unsurprisingly, predominantly positive emotions such as joy, surprise and gratitude lead to the strengthening and affirmation of a positive relationship, while negative emotions affirm the problematic character of a relationship, weaken it or even lead to separation. In contrast, it is a mix of positive and negative emotions that leads to the negligible effect. The observed long-term effect of emotions seems to be more interesting. Apparently, the relationship effect, especially of spontaneous negative emotional reactions, can weaken over time through psychological reinterpretation ("reframing"), because recipients actively downplay and trivialize the incident in their minds (Ruth et al. 1999). This effect may give givers hope for the future development of the relationship in the case of unsuccessful gifts. However, if they truly care about the relationship, they should focus all efforts on making the moment of truth a moment of shared joy.

References

Austin CG, Huang L (2012) First choice? Last resort? Social risks and gift card selection. J Mark Theory Pract 20(39):293–306

Belk RW, Coon GS (1993) Gift giving as agapic love: an alternative to the exchange paradigm based on dating experiences. J Consum Res 20(3):393–417

Berking H (1996) Schenken. Zur Anthropologie des Gebens. Campus Verlag, Frankfurt a. M

Caplow T (1984) Rule enforcement without visible means: Christmas gift giving in Middletown. Am J Sociol 89(6):130–1323

Cheal D (1987) Showing them you love them: gift giving and the dialectic of intimacy. Sociol Rev 35(1):150–169

Clarke J (2007) The four 'S's' of experience gift giving behaviour. Hosp Manag 26:98–116

Clarke JR (2013) Experiential aspects of tourism gift consumption. J Vacat Mark 19(1):75–87

Galak J et al (2016) Why certain gifts are great to give but not to get: a framework for understanding errors in gift giving. Curr Dir Psychol Sci 25(6):380–385

Gino F, Flynn F (2011) Give them what they want: the benefits of explicitness in gift exchange. Adv Consum Res 38:198–199

Hochschild AR (2012) The managed heart. Commercialization of human feeling. University of California Press, Berkeley

Howard D (1992) Gift-wrapping effects on product attitudes: a mood-biasing explanation. J Consum Psychol 1(3):197–223

Otnes C et al (1993) Gift selection for easy and difficult recipients: a social roles interpretation. J Consum Res 20(2):229–244

Paschen M (2018) Weihnachten: Ein Roman, Berlin

Rixom JM et al (2019) Presentation matters: the effect of wrapping neatness on gift attitudes. J Consum Psychol 30(2):329–338

Roster CA (2006) Moments of truth in gift exchanges: a critical incident analysis of communication indicators used to detect gift failure. Psychol Mark 23(11):885–903

Roster CA, Amann CM (2003) Consumer strategies for averting negative consequences of failed gift exchanges: is honesty ever the best policy? Adv Consum Res 30:373–374

Ruth JA et al (1999) Gift receipt and the reformulation of interpersonal relationships. J Consum Res 25(4):385–402

Ruth JA et al (2004) An investigation of the power of emotions in relationship realignment: the gift recipient's perspective. Psychol Mark 21(1):29–52

Sherry JF et al (1992) The disposition of the gift and many unhappy returns. J Retail 68(1):40–65

Taute H, Sierra JJ (2015) An examination of emotional information management in gift giving and receipt. Psychol Mark 32(2):203–218

Yang AX, Urminsky O (2018) The smile-seeking hypothesis: how immediate affective reactions motivate and reward gift giving. Psychol Sci 29(8):1221–1233

12

Gifts and Gender: Santa Claus Is a Woman

Research into gender-specific differences in consumer behaviour has a long tradition. Initially, the reference to gift-giving was only touched upon in rare exceptional cases, but it has increasingly come into focus for some time in the context of public and academic discussions of social gender roles (Fischer and Arnold 1990; Gould and Weil 1991; Rucker et al. 1991, 1994; Otnes et al. 1994; Minowa and Gould 1999; Cleveland et al. 2003; Rugimbana et al. 2003; Mortelmans and Sinardet 2004; Nepomuceno et al. 2016; Minowa et al. 2019).

The starting point and repeated focus of much work is the relatively general observation **that women are much more involved in gift-giving activities than men** and have far more responsibility in this regard. They spend much more time searching for, procuring or creating gifts, they also buy and give more gifts than men (McGrath 1995; Komter and Vollebergh 1997; Mortelmans and Sinardet 2004). When a (married) couple presents a gift to friends or family members together on occasions such as birthdays or Christmas, the fiction of a joint giving activity is often created, when in fact in many cases it is the woman alone who has done the work of selecting, procuring and wrapping (McGrath 1995). In such situations, the man is credited with a gift that he may not even have seen before the recipient unwraps it.

The predominant role of women in gift-giving is particularly evident at Christmas. Caplow's (1982, p. 162) early statement that Christmas shopping is "work of women" is subsequently confirmed by many researchers. According to this statement, women start thinking about suitable gifts earlier and also start shopping earlier in the calendar year. They make sure that everyone is considered and do most of the ritual and preparatory activities such as decorating and mailing (Cheal 1987, 1988; Fischer and Arnold 1990). This is true not only for the United States, for which most empirical studies are available, but for many countries in the Western cultural sphere with Christmas traditions. The symbol of the commercialized Christmas is "Santa Claus," an old man with a white beard who has long prevailed over alternative projections for gift hopes – such as the Christ Child (Stauss 2008). His work, however, is done by women. No wonder Sinardet and Mortelmans (2009) speak of the "feminine side to Santa Claus".

How can we explain the asymmetrical distribution of Christmas preparation and gift-giving work that is consistently described in everyday experience and science? Usually, two interrelated facts are indicated for this: a **gender-specific role allocation and early childhood socialization**. Cheal (1987) points to the traditional family role allocation and division of labour in industrial-capitalist states, where the woman is assigned the place in the domestic sphere of cohabitation and thus given the main responsibility for the family. This responsibility is also expressed

12 Gifts and Gender: Santa Claus Is a Woman

in the value of caring, the personal care and nurturing of children and elderly relatives, which is predominantly seen as a female sphere of responsibility and demarcated against a different kind of masculinity, which in contrast is often defined by professional activity outside the home. In his opinion these values and attitudes can be traced back to children's gender-specific socialisation, in which children learn traditional role patterns and 'gender-defined' behaviours at an early age and girls in particular are taught that caring for others is an important part of the female role.

As plausible as this idea is, doubts arise as to whether it offers sufficient justification. Increasingly, it is being pointed out that the image of society described corresponds less and less to reality and that the role behaviour of men and women in the family has changed considerably. Women's employment outside the home has become the norm, as has a more equal distribution of child- and household-related family work between men and women (Laroche et al. 2000). With regard to caring and nursing activities, a change in the understanding of roles and role behaviour – albeit not as serious – has also been observed. For example, Sinardet and Mortelmans (2009) state that men now make a significant contribution to caring, especially married men who care for their wives in old age and unmarried men who take on the care of a parent. According to the conventional explanation, the observed change in society and roles should also be reflected in giving behaviour, i.e. in a weakening of gender-specific differences. However, this is hardly detectable.

Nevertheless, the results of a study by Fischer and Arnold (1990) indicate a slight change in gender-specific gift-giving behaviour in that a correlation with the degree of attitude towards traditional gender roles can be established. According to this study, men with egalitarian attitudes engage more in Christmas gift-giving activities than those with traditional attitudes, and women with egalitarian views engage (somewhat) less than traditionally oriented women. Nevertheless, this study again confirms that women are on the whole much more involved in Christmas gift-giving activities and also understand and accept this as a serious task, while men are much less involved in these actions and also tend to take them lightly.

A decade later, and thus also after another decade of social change, Laroche et al. (2000) and Cleveland et al. (2003) examine the hypothesis that as women become more employed, differences in gift-giving behavior level off. Specifically, they test the conjecture that women become more like men in behaviour and, more importantly, spend less time searching for information and shopping. However, hypothesis and conjecture do not find confirmation in their studies on women's and men's information-seeking behavior during Christmas shopping. On the contrary, the study confirms the existence of significant gender differences in information seeking at the point of purchase. Women are much more intensive in their search for information and make far greater use of the available information sources in the store. They also start their Christmas shopping much earlier, buy more gifts and make more shopping trips. In contrast, men choose a simpler information process, limit their search to a smaller amount of information, and make less use of available information. From this, the authors conclude that retailers should encourage their salespeople to approach male shoppers relatively soon after they enter the store, but give women more time before offering support or assistance.

A large-scale study by Sinardet and Mortelmans (2009) on gift-giving culture in Belgium, again published about a decade later, also shows a variant of the familiar picture. Despite all the societal changes, substantial gender differences persist. Women remain mainly responsible for the selection and acquisition of gifts. They invest more time in these activities, partly because it is much more important to them to find a gift that fits the recipient perfectly. Moreover, they are quite satisfied with their role, whereby these results are completely independent of the situational circumstances of women's lives or their level of education or income.

This raises the question all the more why the asymmetry of gift-giving behaviour has largely persisted despite societal changes in living conditions and in the understanding of roles. One approach to answering this question is offered by a situation that cannot be seen independently of gender-specific role assignment and early childhood socialisation, but which nevertheless brings a special aspect into focus: "**kin keeping**" (Di Leonardo 1987; Fischer and Arnold 1990). It is usually the women who maintain the inter-household kin relations and make efforts to keep family members in touch. They arrange visits, keep in touch with letters, cards and e-mails, and also provide gifts to ensure that family social relations are maintained and strengthened. In this way, they are both responsible managers and executors of this kinship work. And it seems that it is this almost invisible work that, despite all the otherwise visible role changes, ensures that the traditional distribution of roles is so stable in gift-giving behaviour and is apparently not questioned by women who are satisfied with it (Mortelmans and Damen 2001; Sinardet and Mortelmans 2009). In addition, the term 'kin keeping' does not adequately describe the situation, because in many cases the cultivation of relationships is not limited to relatives, but involves a much larger circle of friends and acquaintances. Incidentally, it is also evident that women cultivate relationships with their female friends particularly intensively and that they give them more gifts than men give their friends. According to Cheal (1987), this observation cannot be traced back to family-related role patterns and nourishes the assumption that there are gender-specific perspectives on relationships that endure despite social changes.

Research findings on gender-specific differences in gift-giving behaviour are available not only on the extent of participation and engagement, but also on a variety of detailed aspects. In the following, selected findings on gender differences are presented with regard to basic attitudes towards gift giving, special gift experiences that are remembered, ideas of what is meant by 'good male or female gifts', and reactions to 'bad' gifts. In addition, results from studies are presented that examine the extent to which corporate promotional activities on gift-giving occasions confirm and reinforce gender stereotypes.

Apparently, men and women have fundamentally different **attitudes towards gift giving**. While a positive attitude clearly predominates among women, men generally have a more negative attitude. For them, giving is much more often associated with terms such as 'stressful' or 'an obligation' (Fischer and Arnold 1990; Wolfinbarger and Gilly 1991). These attitudinal differences are also evident in a projective study by McGrath (1995) in which subjects are asked to write imaginative stories about gift giving. Men tell more negative and unpleasant stories than women. This result, according to the researcher's explanation, could be related to the fact that men feel resentment to participate in a job that, according to cultural norms, women are responsible for, so that gift-giving activities are more threatening for them.

The study by Areni et al. (1998) also shows considerable gender-specific differences, in which male and female participants are asked to describe the experiences with gifts that have **remained most strongly in their memory**. Women predominantly mention experiences in their role as recipients, men as givers. Accordingly, the reasons why they consider gifts to be so memorable also differ greatly. While women primarily recall gifts characterized by special empathy on the part of the giver, men primarily describe their own precise planning, the help they provided with the gift, and the sacrifice they made. Since women are much more involved in gift-giving processes, give much more, and the reasons given by men are usually attributed more to women, the results seem surprising. But the authors plausibly attribute the results to the method used. In the methodological approach used, the Critical Incident Technique, participants are not asked about the typical, everyday experiences, but about the special, the extraordinary experience. Accordingly, the result can be interpreted in such a way that for women the receipt of a particularly carefully and empathically chosen gift is the exception and for men their great commitment in terms of careful planning, help and sacrifice.

Gender differences are particularly evident in the fact that there appear to be different **typical gifts for men and women**. Rucker et al. (1991) found in their exploratory study that people make clear different judgements about what constitutes 'good men's gifts' and 'good women's gifts'. For example, there is widespread agreement that a rose is an appropriate gift for a woman, but not for a man. One did not necessarily need a scientific study to make such assessments, but often actually known facts are only perceived as known by reading them in a different, e.g. scientific, context. And one becomes sensitized to the extent to which these gender-specific differences are considered to be self-evident. Thus it speaks for itself that the feuilleton of a national German daily newspaper describes an opera production as 'fully lived out emancipation', which celebrates its climax in what is obviously perceived as a breaking of taboos with the following headline: 'Sometimes even a woman can give a rose to a man' (Felber 2021).

Interestingly, however, it also happens that men and women evaluate the typical 'good gifts' differently. Thus, in one study it turns out that men evaluate some gifts for women more positively than the women themselves. This applies to sweets, which men see as a desirable "symbol of sweetness" (Rucker et al. 1991, p. 247), while women often classify them as impersonal fatteners. Accordingly, the authors present their research findings in a paper subtitled 'When the sweet don't want sweets'. In such cases, men prove to be insensitive to women's wishes; and since they at the same time think they know quite certainly what women want, the authors speak of a "double jeopardy" of giving an inappropriate gift (Rucker et al. 1991, p. 247).

Men and women also seem to **react** differently **to bad gifts**. According to Dunn et al.'s (2008) studies, there are immediate negative consequences for the relationship when men receive a perceived bad gift. Perceived similarity with their girlfriends decreases, and they express pessimism about the future prospects of the relationship. Such consequences do not occur when women receive unsuccessful gifts. They maintain their positive future prospects for the relationship even in this case. For this result, the authors offer as an explanation that women activate more strongly certain psychological defense mechanisms to avoid threatening the relationship. Alternatively, they point to the possibility that women are simply more forgiving than men. The extent to which these conjectures are correct must remain to be seen. In any case, however, women seem to shield the relationship more strongly against gift shocks than men – a finding that men are likely to note with a sigh of relief (Gupta and Gentry 2019, p. 72).

Some research looks at gender differences in particular gift-giving occasions and the extent to which **corporate advertising promotes gender stereotypes**. Close and Zinkhan (2006) examine gift-giving rituals on Valentine's

Day in the US and find that there are clear differences between members of the two sexes and that market communication clearly reinforces gender roles. More women than men expect (at least) one gift on Valentine's Day, and advertising encourages this by suggesting that the day is primarily about gifting, pampering and showing affection to women. The message to men is thus: buy, buy enough to show your love. Promotional displays, store windows and displays for Valentine's Day gifts are dominated by products for women that men can give and should use as a non-verbal communication of their love. Especially when luxurious gifts are advertised and displayed, men are almost exclusively targeted. Who has ever seen a woman being asked to surprise her sweetheart with a diamond ring on Valentine's Day?

Minowa et al. (2011) examine the understanding and practice of Valentine's Day in Japan based on promotional texts and illustrations in print media over a period of fifty years. This day in Japan is a gift-giving day characterized by particular asymmetry, as on this day only women give gifts to men – mainly chocolate – but not vice versa. It turns out that this day has changed more and more from a simple occasion to show one's affection and strengthen a relationship towards a rite that strengthens women's gender identity.

In a later study, Minowa et al. (2019) focus on gendered rituals of gift-giving on the occasion of White Day in Japan. White Day is a commercially constructed holiday that has been celebrated since the 1980s. It is set for March 14 and serves as a way for men who have received gifts from women on February 14, Valentine's Day, to reciprocate with a return gift that is usually larger. The analysis shows that this day is used by the advertising industry in the media to reinforce conventional expectations of male gender roles through the types of gifts recommended and presented. Thus, White Day gift-giving serves significantly to maintain traditionally typical masculine behaviors and masculine identities and to ward off changes in gendered roles and power relations.

Overall, it appears that the long-lasting change in social roles has only had a comparatively small impact on the gift-giving behaviour of the sexes. As long as firmly anchored and hardly conscious task assignments – such as kinship work to women – exist, which are also predominantly perceived by them not as a burden but as satisfying, and as long as traditional role models also dominate public gift communication, the 'small differences' will continue to be reflected in rather large differences in gift giving.

References

Areni CS et al (1998) Is it better to give than to receive? Exploring gender differences in the meaning of memorable gifts. Psychol Mark 15(1):81–109

Caplow T (1982) Christmas gifts and kin networks. Am Sociol Rev 47(3):383–392

Cheal D (1987) Showing them you love them: gift giving and the dialectic of intimacy. Sociol Rev 35(1):150–169

Cheal D (1988) The gift economy. Routledge, London

Cleveland M et al (2003) Information search patterns for gift purchases: a cross-national examination of gender differences. J Consum Behav 3(1):20–47

Close A, Zinkhan G (2006) A holiday loved and loathed: a consumer perspective of Valentine's day. Adv Consum Res 33:356–365

Di Leonardo M (1987) The female world of cards and holidays: women, families, and the work of kinship. Signs 12(3):440–453

Dunn EW et al (2008) The gift of similarity: how good and bad gifts influence relationships. Soc Cogn 26(4):469–481

Felber G (2021) Es kann ja auch mal die Frau dem Mann eine Rose schenken. https://www.faz.net/aktuell/feuilleton/

buehne-und-konzert/francesca-da-rimini-an-der-deutschen-oper-berlin-17246546.html. Accessed 18 Mar 2021

Fischer E, Arnold SJ (1990) More than a labor of love: gender roles and Christmas gift shopping. J Consum Res 17(3):333–345

Gould SJ, Weil CE (1991) Gift-giving roles and gender self-concepts. Sex Roles 24(9/10):617–637

Gupta A, Gentry JW (2019) If you love me, surprise me. In: Minowa Y, Belk RW (eds) Gifts, romance, and consumer culture. Routledge, New York, pp 65–79

Komter A, Vollebergh W (1997) Gift giving and the emotional significance of family and friends. J Marriage Fam 59(3):747–757

Laroche M et al (2000) Gender differences in information search strategies for a Christmas gift. J Consum Mark 17(6):500–524

McGrath MA (1995) Gender differences in gift exchanges: new directions from projections. Psychol Mark 12(5):371–393

Minowa Y, Gould SJ (1999) Love my gift, love me or is it love me, love my gift: a study of the cultural construction of love and gift-giving among Japanese couples. Adv Consum Res 26:119–124

Minowa Y et al (2011) Social change and gendered gift-giving rituals: a historical analysis of Valentine's day in Japan. J Macromark 31(1):44–56

Minowa Y et al (2019) Practicing masculinity and reciprocation in gendered gift-giving rituals. In: Minowa Y, Belk RW (eds) Gifts, romance, and consumer culture. Routledge, New York, pp 101–125

Mortelmans D, Damen S (2001) Attitudes on commercialisation and anti-commercial reactions on gift giving occasions in Belgium. J Consum Behav 1(2):156–173

Mortelmans D, Sinardet D (2004) The role of gender in gift buying in Belgium. J Fam Consum Sci 96(2):34–39

Nepomuceno M et al (2016) Testosterone & gift-giving: mating confidence moderates the association between digit ratios (2D: 4D and *rel2*) and erotic gift-giving. Pers Individ Diff 91(4):27–30

Otnes C et al (1994) The pleasure and pain of being close: men's mixed feelings about participation in Valentine's day gift exchang. Adv Consum Res 21:159–164

Rucker M et al (1991) Gender stereotypes and gift failures: when the sweet don't want sweets. GCB - Gend Consum Behav 1:244–252

Rucker M et al (1994) A toast for the host? The male perspective on gifts that say thank you. Adv Consum Res 21:165–168

Rugimbana R et al (2003) The role of social power relations in gift giving on Valentine's day. J Consum Behav 3(1):63–73

Sinardet D, Mortelmans D (2009) The feminine side to Santa Claus. Women's work of kinship in contemporary gift-giving relations. Soc Sci J 46(1):124–142

Stauss B (2008) Starke Marke – Dienstleistung. Santa Claus, Christkind und Sankt Nikolaus stehen im Wettbewerb. Der Weihnachtsmann hat als Geschenkebringer die Nase vorn. Rheinischer Merkur – Christ und Welt 49:25

Wolfinbarger MF, Gilly MC (1991) The relationship of gender to gift-giving attitudes (or are men insensitive clods?). GCB – Gend Consum Behav 1:223–233

13

Gifts and Culture: What Applies Globally and What Regionally?

Gift-giving is a cross-cultural and cross-temporal phenomenon, i.e. an exchange ritual that is known in all cultures and all historical periods. This is already made clear by the pioneering ethnographic research on gift-giving in early cultures, for example the studies of Mauss (1990 [1923/1924]) and Malinowski (1984 [1922]) among archaic peoples in the Pacific island groups of Melanesia and Polynesia or among indigenous tribes in Northwest America. Such ethnographic studies have contributed significantly to identifying basic **general principles**, such as, above all, the principles to give, to receive, and to reciprocate. However, they also reveal **specific manifestations**, some of which are extreme in character. An example of this is the potlatch, a ritual gift-giving festival of (mainly) Northwest American indigenous tribes. At this festival, the more valuable and exquisite a gift is, the more givers can maintain and increase their social position and the rank of their lineage. In the resulting competition, competing clans give each other gifts so lavishly until one side can no longer surpass the gift received. This system of gift giving and value destruction can have serious social and economic consequences. Thus, as potlatches were increasingly held, groups were driven into poverty and ruin, leading to the banning of these festivals in Canada and the United States in the late nineteenth century, a ban that remained in effect until the mid-twentieth century.

The field of tension between cross-culturally valid principles and functions of gift-giving on the one hand and regional characteristics and rules of gift-giving behaviour on the other hand continues to exist in a modified form and has attracted increased attention in research in the course of the development towards a largely globalised world economy. With the enormous growth in international economic cooperation, the number of intercultural contacts is also increasing massively. While these are facilitated by international convergence of lifestyles and consumption patterns, cultural differences remain in the sense that different rules and patterns of behavior continue to apply to individuals from different cultural backgrounds. Accordingly, the need for knowledge about values, norms and habits of other cultures increases in order to be able to behave adequately in intercultural professional, but also private contacts.

In the practical business context, this need for knowledge has led to a boom in works on **intercultural management**. They not only deal with topics of internal intercultural cooperation such as leadership, organizational development or teamwork, but also provide information on cultural peculiarities to be observed in private and everyday situations: Greeting and farewell rituals, dress norms, forms of verbal and non-verbal communication – and rules for giving and receiving gifts. The classic handbook for US managers operating internationally, tellingly titled "Kiss, bow, or shake hands" and advertised as a "Passport to International

13 Gifts and Culture: What Applies Globally...

Business Etiquette", contains tips on proper behaviour in 61 countries (plus Hong Kong). And although there are only a few pages for each country, including information on the historical and political background, value systems, business practices and common negotiating styles, each chapter also contains a section on manners, in which the topic of "gifts" is dealt with in a separate sub-chapter alongside aspects such as greeting rituals, body language or dress code (Morrisson and Conaway 2006). Here, for example, one learns details about

- Colors: among others, no black or purple, symbolizing mourning (Brazil),
- Types of flowers: including no chrysanthemums (Belgium) or white lilies (UK), which represent death; no red roses, which are reserved for lovers (Germany),
- Flowers, number: among others, odd number, no 13 (Czech Republic),
- Flowers, delivery: send beforehand (Portugal), remove paper of a bouquet before delivery (Sweden),
- Religious affiliation of the recipient: kosher (Israel) or halal food (Muslim countries), no leather products (to Hindus),
- Type of delivery: giving and receiving with both hands (China), with the right hand (Egypt, Israel),
- Time of opening the package: immediately after receipt (Chile), not in the presence of the donor (India, Singapore).

But these are only rough indications. For a precise insight into the meaning and nature of the respective gift-giving culture, further sources must be consulted. For Japan, for example, these provide information on the religious origins and aims of gift-giving, the approximately 50 different gift-giving occasions, the reciprocity principle 'giri', the traditionally popular gifts on certain occasions (on Valentine's Day, only men receive gifts – usually chocolate) or the need for particularly careful and beautiful packaging in precious cloths or fine paper in the right colour, avoiding black and white in particular (Grinko 2021).

With the help of this kind of information, one can reduce the risk that gifts will fail in intercultural contacts. However, a high degree of forgiveness can still be expected, at least in the case of initial misbehaviour. Findings on international service encounters show that violations of cultural norms in personal contact do not necessarily lead to "culture shocks" with negative consequences, as long as the incident is attributed to ignorance of cultural customs. However, if it is assumed that the person concerned knows or should know the norm, there is no longer any excuse, and the partner reacts (usually inwardly) not with forgiveness but with reproach (Stauss and Mang 1999; Stauss 2016).

Management-oriented books and media are dominated by detailed descriptions of culturally shaped gift-giving rituals and norms in individual countries, usually combined with recommendations for their respectful observance. Psychological research, on the other hand, is concerned in greater depth with the investigation of fundamental similarities and differences in the gift-giving behaviour of different **cultures**. In particular, comparisons are made between the attitudes, rules and practices in Western and East Asian countries.

This comparison is based on the groundbreaking work of Hofstede and Hall, who diagnosed a particularly large cultural distance between these two cultures. Hofstede (1980) typologises country cultures according to the dimensions of 'power distance', 'individualism/collectivism', 'masculinity' and 'uncertainty avoidance'. Western countries can be characterised by low power distance (norm of equal distribution of power and equal social relations), individualism (priority of one's own personality), low masculinity (less clearly defined gender roles) and low uncertainty avoidance (encouragement to take risks and pragmatic handling of rules). In contrast, the following dimensions are characteristic of Eastern cultures: high power distance (acceptance of the unequal distribution of power and associated hierarchies), collectivism (high degree of group integration), high masculinity (clear and different assignment of gender roles), and uncertainty avoidance (perception of uncertain situations as threatening).

Hall (1976) has introduced the distinction between "high-context" and "low-context" cultures into the discussion, focusing primarily on the nature of communication. For high-context cultures of the East it is typical that messages are communicated by means of material things and non-verbally, whereas in low-context cultures of the West explicit and specified verbal communication is common.

These cultural differences have a variety of consequences in terms of gift-giving behaviour, with empirical comparative studies mainly referring to Hofstede's distinction between individualistic and collectivistic cultures and Hall's context concept.

The consequences of belonging to an **individualistic or collectivistic culture** for gift-giving behaviour arise above all with regard to the assigned significance of gifts as a medium of information, the ideas of the right or perfect gift and the relevance of the reciprocity rule.

Belonging to an individualistic or collectivistic culture obviously influences decisions about **the type of gift**. In Western countries, people tend to see themselves as independent individuals, they want to gear their gift to the specific personality of the recipient and often use it as a medium of self-expression at the same time. Accordingly, they look for **differentiated**, if possible unique gifts. In contrast, people from East Asian cultures prefer **standard**

gifts that emphasize and publicize their attachment to traditional customs in the group (Beichen and Murshed 2015; Chinchanachokchai and Pusaksrikit 2019). Cultural influence is also evident in terms of the choice between gifts in kind and experiential gifts. **Experiential gifts** such as a restaurant visit, concert tickets, or travel allow for specific shared experiences that are hard to compare with alternatives. They are especially attractive to people from individualistic cultures who seek and highly value specific hedonistic pleasures. In contrast, people from collectivist cultures place more value on **material gifts** that have value and remain in the possession of the recipient. Brand names and luxurious products play a prominent role in this regard, as they are considered visible evidence of the elevated social status and therefore provide social recognition (Chinchanachokchai and Pusaksrikit 2019).

This already indicates that the ideas of the '**perfect gift**' also differ. Belk's (1996) definition and description of the 'perfect gift' originate from the Western cultural sphere, and even if essential characteristic properties have cross-cultural significance, there are still culture-specific characteristics and weightings. This also applies to the most important dimensions of the symbolic value of gifts, empathy, sacrifice and effort, and surprise.

Empathy and recipient orientation are also significant in the East Asian region, but more important than the wishes and needs of the recipient is the aspect of saving face, which is deeply rooted in the traditional culture and strongly influences gift-giving behavior (Liu et al. 2010). A gift communicates important information about the identity of both the giver and the receiver, and it is therefore necessary to find a gift that ensures that the face of both parties is preserved in all aspects. This requires that the image of the gift be consistent with the image the giver wants to create of him/herself in the eyes of others (social self-image), and with the self-image of the recipient. In their studies with Chinese subjects, Liu et al. (2010) are able to demonstrate that the consistency between the gift image with the giver's social self-image positively influences the giver's intention to buy this gift. And this effect is more pronounced the more the respondents share traditional Chinese values. These include a focus on interpersonal, interdependent relationships, the pursuit of a balance between personal and group interests, the recognition of social hierarchies and compliance with existing rules, norms and constraints.

Sacrifice and effort are features of good gifts in both cultures, but this seems to be interpreted and weighted differently. In Eastern cultures, it is primarily the financial sacrifices that count, especially high expenditures made, for example, to purchase expensive brand-name and luxury items. Of lesser importance, on the other hand, are the time and effort spent on making gifts oneself. This is because these are much less suitable as status symbols and can hardly be quantified financially in terms of the required countergift (Rucker et al. 1996).

There are also strong differences with regard to the evaluation of **surprises**. While people from Western cultures predominantly believe that a perfect gift should surprise, people from Eastern cultures, which are also characterised by the pursuit of uncertainty avoidance, do not share this view. For them, predictability, balance, and emotional control are important, so surprises are little valued (Rucker et al. 1996).

Not all cross-cultural comparative studies confirm these differences. Minowa and Gould (1999) identify the most memorable gift experiences of Japanese men and women, both as givers and recipients. As a result, they find a high degree of correspondence between remembered gift experiences and Western-style understandings of the perfect gift. For example, a home-knitted sweater is perceived by men as luxurious in the sense of not being interchangeable, as a result of the investment of time and effort, and as surprising. The authors offer the following explanation for this divergent result: Unlike other studies, they focused solely on gift-giving experiences of romantic couples, which allows the participants to express their personal feelings in private and to deviate from general cultural norms.

All comparative studies emphasize that the **reciprocity rule** is of very special importance in East Asian culture. It is based on traditional cultural values of Confucianism, Buddhism and Taoism and has been an integral part of the philosophy of life for centuries. These include, for example, the Japanese traditional system of rules 'Giri', which is based on the moral obligation to reciprocate, or the Chinese network of personal relationships 'Guanxi', which consists of an endless cycle of mutual favours. They fulfill important social functions. They serve to recognize and promote relationships of kinship and friendship, to secure status and save face, and to reduce conflicts. In this respect, the rule of strictly 'balanced' reciprocity applies – with regard to the financial value of a gift, but also with regard to being owed a favour in the future. Any refusal to reciprocate appropriately is associated with loss of face and a deterioration of the relationship (Rucker et al. 1996; Yau et al. 1999; D'Souza 2003; Qian et al. 2007). Since in Asian culture there is a much stronger distinction between "ingroup" and "outgroup" than in the West, this is especially true for the regular and closer relationships in the ingroup. In relation to members of the outgroup, the strong reciprocity rule can also mean that Asians are more likely to reject smaller gifts from casual acquaintances if they do not see an opportunity to respond very easily and quickly with a counter-gift (Shen et al. 2011).

Another difference lies in the **importance of money** or the price of a gift. This is very clearly shown by a

Chinese-German comparative study (Peng 2016). The survey results show that the Chinese involved consider money and thus also more expensive gifts to be an important indicator of closeness in the relationship to a much greater extent, so that the price and not the good intention is decisive for the gift evaluation by the giver and recipient. This is also evident from the fact that the Chinese provide far more information about the price of the gift than Germans in order to emphasize its importance. The greatest difference between the groups of subjects relates to the question of whether – invited to the birthday party – they would give their boss an expensive gift. The Chinese affirm this question to a far greater extent than the Germans, which is explained by the stronger expression of the cultural dimension of power distance with the acceptance of hierarchies, but also of the traditional norm 'guanxi' of maintaining relationships characterised by reciprocity.

While these works primarily use the "individualism-collectivism" cultural dimension identified by Hofstede to explain differences in gift-giving behaviour, other authors focus primarily on the **differentiation between "low-context" and "high-context" cultures**. In general, Hanna and Srivastava (2015) see the strong influence of high-context culture as the main reason why gift giving is a much more complex issue in Japan than in Western countries. The more non-verbal communication is not only reflected in the value of material gifts, but also in the importance of the packaging and the subtle indirect gestures during the handover. A comparative study of gift-giving in romantic relationships with American and Chinese participants underscores differences of this nature. Beichen and Murshed (2015) examine how cultural environment affects whether romantic love is expressed more verbally or through gifts. As a result, it is found that Chinese subjects express their love more with gifts, while Americans express it more with words. The authors explain this result by saying that in Western cultures, where more emphasis is placed on individuality and self-expression is comparatively common, the open verbal articulation of feelings is also natural. In contrast, in the collectivist cultures of East Asia, there is a pronounced tendency toward harmony and balance, as well as a prevailing expectation to demonstrate compliance with social norms through concrete behavior rather than primarily through words. In addition, there is no encouragement to show feelings publicly. Therefore, romantic feelings are also expressed less verbally than through gifts, which serve as concrete and material symbols of love.

All these research findings show that the cultural influence on gift-giving behaviour is strong and diverse. Relevance and dominance of cultural influence can be demonstrated even where people live in places with very different cultural influences or even in a different cultural setting. Such evidence is provided, for example, by Joy (2001) in his analysis of gift-giving behaviour in Hong Kong. In this former British Crown Colony and current Special Administrative Region with strong international economic activity, various cultural influences are at work, but the values and norms embedded in Chinese culture clearly play a crucial role and determine gift-giving behavior. In their studies, Rucker et al. (1994) compare the behavior of American and Japanese-born college students in the United States and diagnose clear differences, for example, in the selection of gifts in accordance with the culture with which the respondents identify. For example, students of Japanese descent prefer food as a gift, while White American students prefer alcohol. Similarly, Aung et al.'s (2017) study of Chinese immigrants in Canada shows that while partial adaptations occur, for example, the acceptance of special gift-giving occasions (such as Christmas, Valentine's Day, Father's Day, and Mother's Day), important traditional cultural values retain influence when it comes to actual gifting behaviour.

Culturally determined differences in gift-giving behaviour are also shown by studies in which the subjects come from cultures with much less cultural distance than is the case in the prevailing West-East discussion. This is shown, for example, by Laroche et al.'s (2000) comparative study of Christmas gift buying among Anglophone and Francophone residents of the Canadian province of Quebec, who differ not only in language but also in customs, traditions, and religious affiliation. Indeed, these cultural differences also influence aspects of Christmas gift-giving, particularly information-seeking behaviour, as French Canadians, among others, are more likely to seek contact with sales staff than their Anglophone counterparts.

Despite their large number and the extensive consistency of the results, such intercultural comparative studies must be interpreted with caution. This is because it is fundamentally problematic to draw conclusions about cultural differences between countries or even cross-national cultures from surveys with relatively few respondents, who also often come from a specific milieu (students). On the one hand, this applies because the respective national cultures of a cultural group under consideration are by no means homogeneous – for example, the East Asian cultures of China, Japan, Thailand or Korea differ considerably. On the other hand, even cultures within a country are becoming increasingly heterogeneous in the course of global migration.

Because of the **increasing cultural diversity** and the development of social subcultures, there are also more and more domestic intercultural contacts in networks of friendship, neighbourhoods and families. And then intercultural questions of giving also arise 'at home' and quite concretely, above all when religious aspects are at the same time affected. Many Muslims who now live in a country with

Christian traditions and customs and at the same time want to act according to their faith ask themselves these questions or articulate them on religious-Muslim websites or in social media: Are Muslims allowed to accept an invitation for a birthday, are they allowed to give someone a present or to accept gifts at Christmas, are they allowed to wish Merry Christmas or even to return such a greeting? On relevant websites with religious answers for Muslims, harsh prohibitions are usually communicated and corresponding behaviours are described as sins and betrayals of the religion. On the other hand, there are also many liberal voices that, for example, accept Christmas as less religious and more as a cross-cultural celebration and allow certain adaptations as an expression of desired integration. Important Muslim associations in Germany also turn to Christian communities, neighbours and friends with good wishes for reflective Christmas days (Islam 2020). But the situation remains ambivalent, complicated, in need of explanation and uncertain for givers and receivers. This is especially true for families where different cultural and/or religious backgrounds, traditions, norms and expectations are intimately intertwined. Gift-giving in such domestic and familial intercultural constellations has so far been completely neglected academically. How good that fiction is opening our eyes to this problem.

In the novel "Weihnachten" ('Christmas') by Maruan Paschen, presented in Chap. 11, the narrator is the son of a German mother and a Palestinian father whom he has never met. One Christmas, an – actually benevolent – uncle gives him a dictionary for Canac-German, German-Canac, which everyone finds funny, except the recipient, the narrator. For in Germany 'canac' is used with an derogatory connation against people with family roots in oriental countries. No wonder he tears up the book in the car on the way home with his mother. After his mother told the uncle that they did not agree with the gift, the uncle gave him a German-Arabic, Arabic-German dictionary at the next opportunity. The presentee also tore up this gift (Paschen 2018). Another example of gift-giving problems in culturally diverse families can bei found in Sarah Khan's story "Weihnachten mit Hüsniye" ('Christmas with Hüsniye").

> **Sarah Khan: Weihnachten mit Hüsniye (Christmas with Hüsniye)**
>
> Sarah Khan's autobiographical narrative is strongly influenced by her own childhood longing for Christmas and the feeling of not really belonging. Sarah Khan is the daughter of a German mother and a Pakistani father and therefore grew up in and between different cultures. After spending her early years with her parents in her grandfather's pastorate of a Protestant church in Hamburg, she later lived with her father, initially a single parent after her mother left, and then together with her Pakistani stepmother, whom her father had unexpectedly married during a business trip.
> Sarah loved Christmas, which was celebrated in the tolerant and turbulent atmosphere of the extended family with many uncles and aunts in the Lutheran pastorate, and always regretted it when her father, who did not issue any religiously motivated prohibitions but did not feel comfortable with the celebration, always urged to leave rather quickly. In the extended family Sarah was welcome, and she received gifts lovingly chosen – often by the grandfather's new wife. For example, she received a number of books for young people that focused on the fate of foreign children, such as Afghan girls, Indian orphans, or Turkish street children. Books that, from Sarah's point of view, had no relation to her life and – even worse – were perceived primarily as evidence of her foreignness in the family. So even well-intentioned gifts, chosen with the specific 'cultural' situation in mind, can fail (Khan 2018).

Insights into the culture-specific shaping of everyday behaviour and thus also of gift-giving are important for the development of our intercultural understanding and the avoidance of misunderstandings in commercial and private encounters outside the borders of our country. But more important still are the issues arising from the development towards a multi-cultural society in our closest environment. These include changes in customs and celebrations where all can participate as much as possible without feeling excluded or overwhelmed, and where they exchange gifts with family members, friends, and neighbors with cultural empathy. It is to be hoped that gift research will also devote itself to answering these questions in the future.

References

Aung M et al (2017) The evolving gift-giving practices of bicultural consumers. J Consum Mark 34(1):43–52

Beichen L, Murshed F (2015) Culture, expressions of romantic love, and gift-giving. J Int Bus Res 14(1):68–84

Belk RW (1996) The perfect gift. In: Otnes C, Beltramini RF (eds) Gift giving: a research anthology. Bowling Green State University Popular Press, Bowling Green, pp 59–85

Chinchanachokchai S, Pusaksrikit T (2019) 5 Characteristics and meanings of good and bad romantic gifts across cultures. A recipient's perspective. In: Minowa Y, Belk RW (eds) Gifts, romance, and consumer culture. Routledge, New York, pp 80–98

D'Souza CD (2003) An inference of gift-giving within Asian business culture. Asia Pac J Mark Logistics 15(1):27–39

Grinko M (2021) Die japanische Geschenkkultur – Geben und Nehmen. https://oryoki.de/blog/japanische-geschenkkultur/. Accessed 3 Mar 2021

Hall ET (1976) Beyond culture. Anchor Books, New York

Hanna N, Srivastava T (2015) Cultural aspects of gift giving: a comparative analysis of the significance of gift giving in the U.S. and Japan. In: Sidin S, Manrai A (eds) Proceedings of the 1997 world marketing congress. Developments in marketing science: proceedings of the academy of marketing science. Springer, Cham, pp 283–287

Hofstede G (1980) Culture's consequences: international differences in work-related values. Sage Publications, Beverly Hills

Islam (2020) Islamische Religionsgemeinschaften beglückwünschen zu Weihnachten. https://www.islamiq.de/2020/12/24/islamische-religionsgemeinschaften-beglueckwuenschen-zu-weihnachten/. Accessed 3 Apr 2021

Joy A (2001) Gift giving in Hong Kong and the continuum of social ties. J Consum Res 28:239–256

Khan S (2018) Weihnachten mit Hüsniye. mikrotext, Berlin

Laroche M et al (2000) A cross-cultural study of in-store information search strategies for a Christmas gift. J Bus Res 49(2):113–126

Liu S et al (2010) Moderating effect of cultural values on decision making of gift-giving from a perspective of self-congruity theory: an empirical study from Chinese context. J Consum Mark 27(7):604–614

Malinowski B (1984) Argonauts of the western Pacific: an accoujnt of native enterprise and adventure in the Archipelagoes of Melanesian New Guinea. Waveland Press, Prospect Heights

Mauss M (1990) The gift: the forms and reasons for exchange in archaic societies. Routledge, London

Minowa Y, Gould SJ (1999) Love my gift, love me or is it love me, love my gift: a study of the cultural construction of love and gift-giving among Japanese couples. Adv Consum Res 26:119–124

Morrisson T, Conaway WA (2006) Kiss, bow, or shake hands, 2nd edn. Adams, Avon

Paschen M (2018) Weihnachten: Ein Roman. MSB Matthes & Seitz, Berlin

Peng M (2016) A contrastive study of gift-giving between Chinese and Germans. US-China Foreign Lang 14(8):597–604

Qian W et al (2007) Chinese cultural values and gift-giving behavior. J Consum Mark 24(4):214–228

Rucker MH et al (1994) A toast for the host? The male perspective on gifts that say thank you. Adv Consum Res 21:165–168

Rucker MH et al (1996) The role of ethnic identity in gift giving. In: Otnes C, Beltramini RF (eds) Gift giving: a research anthology. Bowling Green State University Popular Press, Bowling Green, pp 143–159

Shen H et al (2011) Cross-cultural differences in the refusal to accept a small gift: the differential influence of reciprocity norms on Asians and North Americans. J Pers Soc Psychol 100(2):271–281

Stauss B (2016) Retrospective: "culture shocks" in inter-cultural service encounters? J Serv Mark 30(4):377–383

Stauss B, Mang P (1999) "Culture shocks" in inter-cultural service encounters? J Serv Mark 13(4/5):329–346

Yau OHM et al (1999) Influence of Chinese cultural values on consumer behaviour. A proposed model of gift-purchasing behaviour in Hong Kong. J Int Consum Mark 11(1):97–116

Epilogue

That it is difficult to give the perfect gift is something everyone has experienced. After reading the findings of psychological gift research summarized in this book, it seems downright impossible. Obviously, whether a recipient considers a gift perfect depends on too many influencing factors, including his or her expectations, interests, and taste preferences, as well as the nature and intensity of the relationship, all of which are not constant in character but subject to dynamic change. There is no panacea that can safely prevent a recipient from perceiving a gift as too cheap or too expensive, too useful, too trivial, off-taste, or as violating milieu- and culture-specific values, or from missing out on the giver's thoughtful, time-consuming, and personal efforts and sacrifices.

In view of this observation, is it not better to do without gifts altogether? Time and again, people see the solution to all the problems mentioned above in foregoing gifts and make a corresponding agreement – especially with regard to Christmas – in the sense of "This time we really won't give each other any presents". At first glance, this seems reasonable, stress-avoiding, cost-effective and sustainable. In fact, however, such an agreement turns out to be much more risky than gift-giving. Not only are gifts information media, but not giving a gift also contains a message, namely that the parties involved simply no longer feel like, or no longer consider it worth the effort, to think about what the other person might want or could make happy. A message that gives the relationship a damning report card. In addition, experience shows that this agreement is almost always broken, which only ends comparatively smoothly if both partners do not keep to the agreement or are prepared for the fact that the other breaks the agreement. But if only one stands there without a gift, then the recipient cannot accept the gift, which really should not be, with joy, but feels himself shabby and betrayed by the other. Even a not particularly perfect gift cannot have a worse effect.

So we will continue to give gifts in the future, and the defined characteristics of the ideal concept of the perfect gift help us to reduce the risk of failure. With empathy for the person of the recipient, with appropriate consideration of the situation, occasion and current state of the relationship, with thought, commitment and care, it will be possible in most cases to please the recipient. This also applies to cases where certain requirements of a perfect gift cannot be met because, for example, the recipient's wishes are largely unknown, the recipient does not express any wishes either, or has such precise expectations that a surprise is impossible. So it is quite conceivable that the hardly known niece is really thrilled about a sum of money for self-determined use, that the actually wish-less uncle reacts to a voucher for a joint visit to a restaurant with joyful surprise, and the partner is relieved and happy that there was no nasty surprise because his or her precisely articulated wish was actually fulfilled.

Therefore, gifts that have all the characteristics of a perfect gift will tend to be the exception, despite your best efforts, but you can make sure that failed gifts are the far greater exception.

Moreover, it should be borne in mind that the gifts we rate as perfect at the moment of receipt need by no means be the ones we remember as the most important. In their studies "The 'perfect gift' and the 'best gift ever'" Branco-Illodum and Heath investigate which gifts are stored in memory as the "best gift ever". The characteristics of the ideal perfect gift certainly play a role, but the emotional value, which is not necessarily fully perceived at the moment of handing over the real gift, goes far beyond that. According to the researchers' findings, such gifts perceived as particularly precious can be characterised by one of three – overlapping – features: They are experiential, life changing, and unforgettable. Thus, it is often not the received objects themselves that are decisive for the indelible memory, but the accompanying circumstances, one's own life situation and the people involved. There are the special occasions, the key moments and turning points in life, which symbolize, for example, gifts for a successful graduation from school or for moving into one's first own apartment. Or the objects are mentally and emotionally inseparable from loved ones, such as the first gift from a future husband or the last gift given by a grandmother who has since passed away. It is quite conceivable that such gifts are perceived as outstanding only in retrospect, that one recognizes the importance of a specific moment in life and the significance of a person for one's own personality development only much later and in retrospect. In such cases, one will also regret it if the memorable and often remembered "best gift ever" is long gone.

When a perfect gift is given, it is a stroke of luck for both recipient and giver; when a gift turns out to be the best gift ever for the recipient, it represents an even rarer stroke of luck. The characteristics attributed to the perfect gift provide important clues as to how we should proceed if we want to bring joy and avoid disappointment with the gift. The characteristics of the "best gift ever" offer little planning guidance to the giver, but they point out with great clarity that gifts can be essential tangible triggers of intangible memories of moments and people. We should therefore not important moments of the lives of people we care about pass us by without a gift; and we should keep in mind the requirements of a perfect gift if we want to be remembered well.

GPSR Compliance
The European Union's (EU) General Product Safety Regulation (GPSR) is a set of rules that requires consumer products to be safe and our obligations to ensure this.

If you have any concerns about our products, you can contact us on

ProductSafety@springernature.com

In case Publisher is established outside the EU, the EU authorized representative is:

Springer Nature Customer Service Center GmbH
Europaplatz 3
69115 Heidelberg, Germany

www.ingramcontent.com/pod-product-compliance
Lightning Source LLC
LaVergne TN
LVHW012009260326
834688LV00057B/355